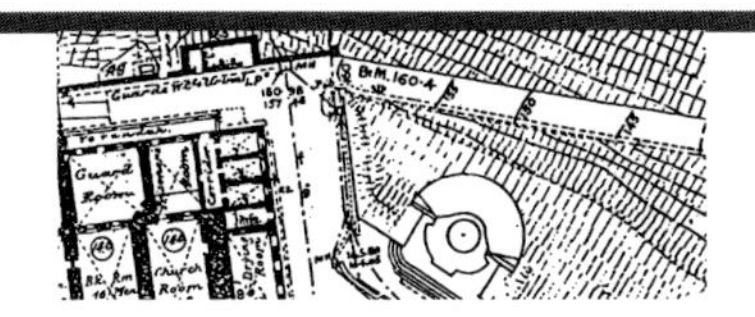

The Archaeology of Cork City and Harbour

from the Earliest Times to Industrialisation

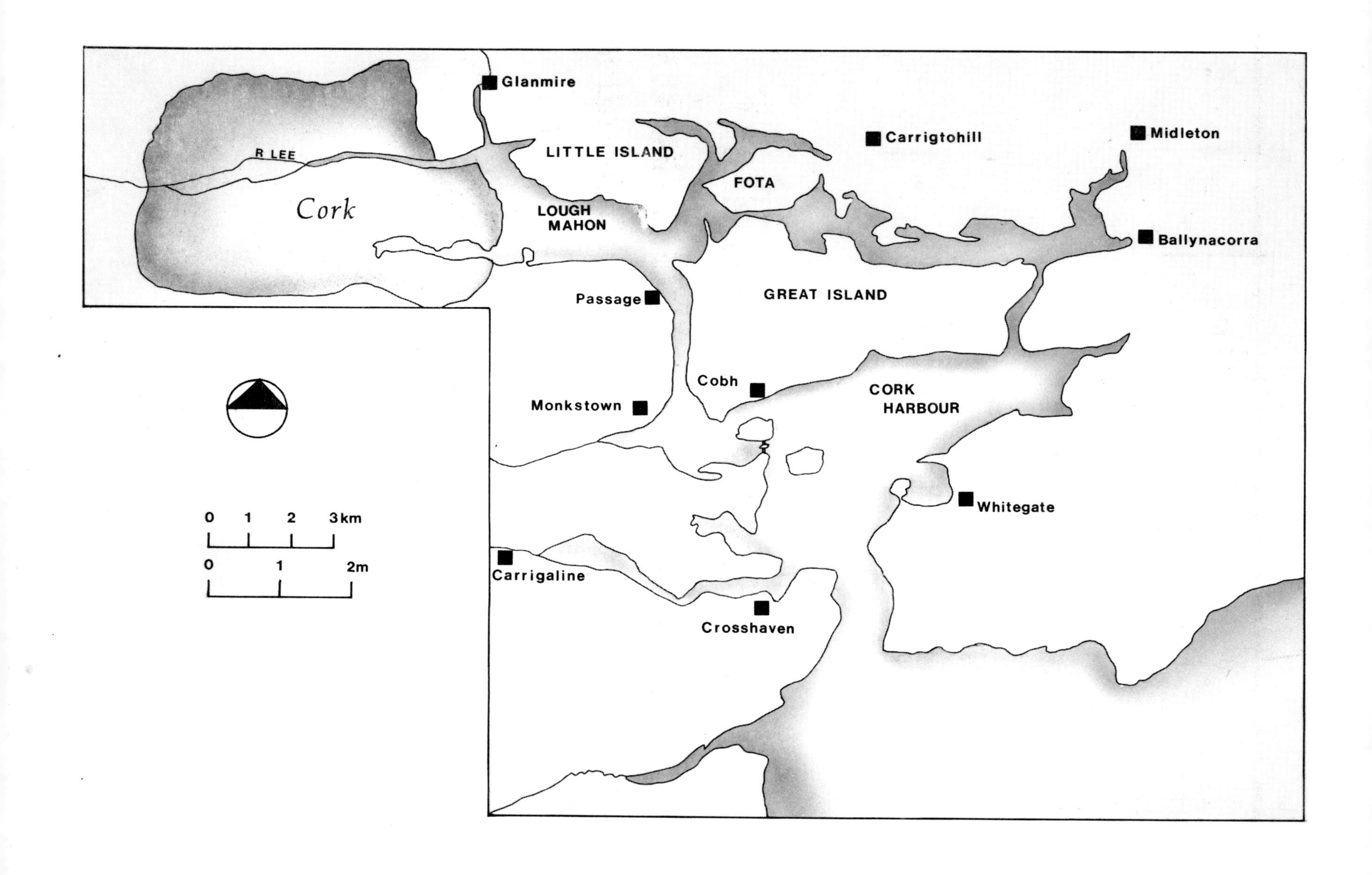
Glanmire
Midleton
Carrigtohill
R LEE
LITTLE ISLAND
FOTA
Cork
LOUGH
MAHON
Ballynacorra
Passage
GREAT ISLAND
Cobh
CORK
HARBOUR
Monkstown
Whitegate
0 1 2 3km
0 1 2m
Carrigaline
Crosshaven

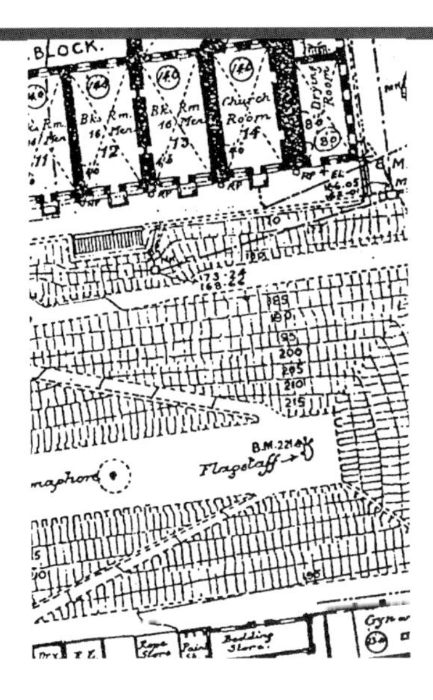

The Archaeology of Cork City and Harbour

from the Earliest Times to Industrialisation

Colin Rynne

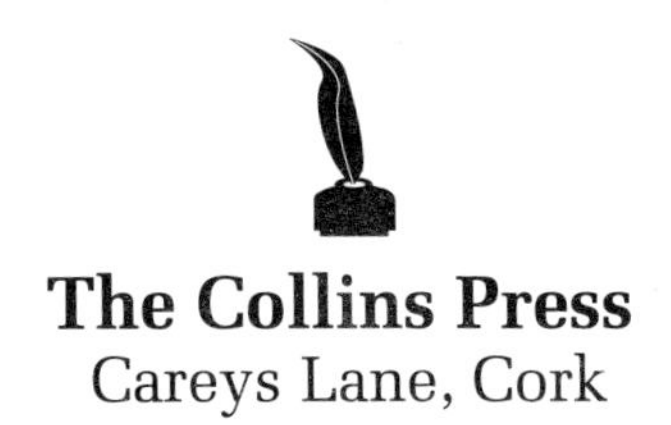

The Collins Press
Careys Lane, Cork

Published by
The Collins Press, Carey's Lane, Cork.

Printed in Ireland by
Colour Books Ltd., Dublin.

Book Design by Upper Case Ltd., Cork
Typeset by Upper Case Ltd., Cork.

ISBN-0-95130368-X

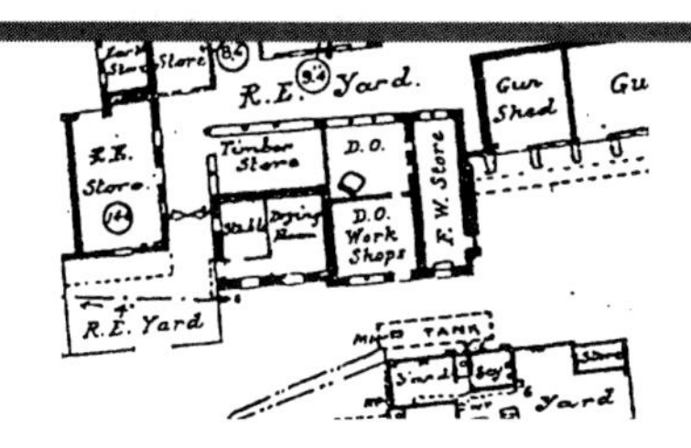
R.E. Yard.
Gun Shed
Timber Store
D.O.
D.O. Work Shops
R.W. Store
R.E. Store
R.E. Yard
Yard

Contents

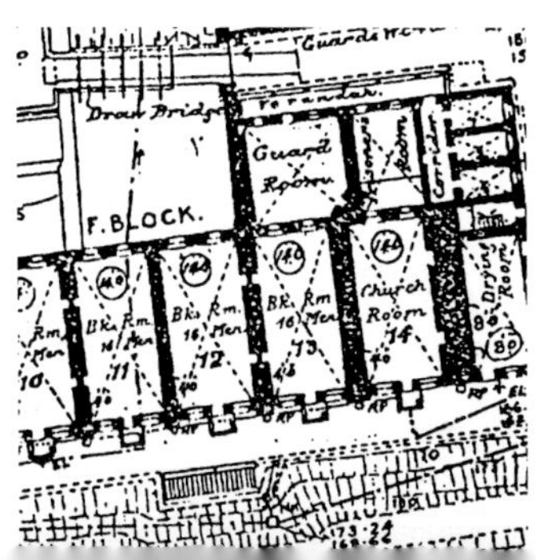
Draw Bridge
Guard Room
F. BLOCK.
Church Room

List of Illustrations

Figure numbers and captions

Acknowledgements

Books of this kind are nearly always summaries of the work of others. It is my great pleasure to acknowledge my debt to the goodwill of the many people who lent their expertise and gave advice, without which the completion of this book would not have been possible.

Mr Denis Power, Director of the Cork Archaeological Survey (based at University College, Cork) and the Survey archaeologists Liz Byrne, Ursula Egan, Sheila Lane, Mrs. Judith Monk and Mary Sleman, for access to the survey archives, photographic material and welcome advice on the archaeology of the greater Cork area; Ms. Stella Cherry, Curator, Cork Public Museum (and formerly of the National Museum of Ireland) for undertaking essential research on artefacts from the Cork area in the collections of the National Museum of Ireland and for permission to reproduce photographs of the Cork Horns; Dr. Pat Wallace, Director of the National Museum of Ireland, for permission to produce photographs of artefacts in the Museum's collections and Ms. Valerie Dowling for the excellent photographic work which made this possible; the Management Committee of the Royal Irish Academy Industrial Archaeological Survey of Cork City and its Environs - Prof. Gordon Herries Davies, Dr. Terry Barry, Mr. David Sweetman and Ms. Mairead Dunleavy- for permission to reproduce material from the survey's archive; Prof. Peter Woodman, and Mr. Michael Monk, Dept. of Archaeology, U.C.C., for discussing aspects of the work in hand with me; Dr. Elizabeth Shee-Twohig, Dept. of Archaeology, U.C.C., for the use of photographic material relating to the Christchurch excavations in Cork city; Ms Anne Marie Lennon, for information and photographic material relating to her excavations at Grattan Street in Cork city and at Raheens near Crosshaven; Mr. Maurice Hurley, City Archaeologist, Cork Corporation, for discussing his important Kyrl's Quay/North Main Street excavations with me and for the use of photographic material; Mr Ewan Rutter and Ms. Patricia O'Connell for information on their recent Fota Island excavations; Ms Martha Hannon and Mr. John Tierney of the Archaeological Services Unit, U.C.C., for information on the environmental remains recovered from the Grattan Street Excavations; Mr Brendan Kelleher (Head County Planner), Mr. John Ludlow (Executive Planner) and Mr Michael Rice (Senior Draughtsman) of Cork County Council for photographic material and survey drawings relating to Ballincollig Gunpowder Mills, Rossleague Martello Tower, Fort Camden and Barryscourt Castle; Mr Kevin Dwyer for photographic work at Barryscourt Castle and Rossleague; Mr. Ciaran Hoare, Upper Case, Cork and Mr Flor Hurley.

The thriving state of local studies within the Cork area is in no small way a consequence of the excellence of the library services provided by the County and City authorities and by University College Cork. In particular, I am grateful to acknowledge the invaluable help of Mr. Ciaran Burke of Cork City Library, Mr. Tim Cadogan, Cork County Library, Ms. Patricia McCarthy, Cork Archives Institute, and Mrs Pat Connolly and Mrs Helen Moloney-Davies of the Library, U.C.C.

Introduction

In recent years the general reader, to some an almost mythical personage, has begun to be properly served by the authors of books on archaeology. These are often referred to as "popular" accounts, which on the face of it may seem conceited, especially if one considers that some of these may not prove as popular with the book-buying public as the use of the word would suggest. Perhaps we should not confuse acceptability with popularity, for although the amateur study of archaeology is undoubtedly both, some of the general accounts which appear from time to time may prove to be neither. Fortunately, where Irish archaeology has been concerned, many of the more recent accounts have successfully addressed the needs of the non-specialist. The present introduction to the archaeology of Cork city and harbour is aimed at the same audience, and to this end I have endeavoured to travel light: I hope that the reader will find the bare minimum of archaeological "baggage" within its pages.

The histories of Cork city and harbour have been inextricably linked by a complex series of circumstances, both natural and man-made, which led to the creation of the entity we now call the port of Cork. It was certainly recognised as such by the early medieval period, and, by the Viking period, it was clearly linked into an extensive trade network. In the succeeding Anglo-Norman period the patchwork of low marshy islands upon which the city of Cork is built became a walled town, a colonial outpost of Norman empire. But only in comparatively recent times did it begin to eclipse the importance of other county Cork ports such as Kinsale and Youghal, neither of which could compete with the considerable advantages which nature had bestowed on Cork harbour. As the subsequent development of the port of Cork was to show, there were no physical restraints to expansion of the city's quaysides as, for example, was the case in nearby Kinsale. The port of Cork also became the focus for much of eighteenth-century English and Irish transatlantic trade, some aspects of which Cork came to dominate outright. It became the main British naval base in Ireland, a circumstance which brought considerable economic gain to Cork merchants. This, in turn, increased its strategic importance to the British navy, not only as the most important transatlantic shipping port, but as a forward post in the defence of the western approaches to England. Cork harbour became one of the most heavily fortified within these Islands, and in becoming so a whole new dimension was added to its traditional role as a safe haven for shipping.

In archaeological terms Cork harbour is not an easy area to define. Strictly speaking it is an expanse of water, but it is, of course, the areas of human settlement around it which are of interest to the archaeologist. But how should we attempt to define these areas? For the purposes of this book I have let the Ordnance Survey settle the matter for me: I have simply chosen the seven, six-inch O.S. maps (sheets 74, 75, 76, 87, 88, 99, and 100) which cover the entire harbour area and the main areas of settlement immediately adjacent to it. All of the archaeological sites referred to in this book can be found on these maps. Inevitably, I have been forced to exclude a number of important sites which lie beyond these artificial boundaries, but in a book of this size and scope there must be a clearly defined cut-off point. This may not be to everyone's liking, but even within this area there are a large number of sites, each of which cannot be described separately in a general book such as this. I have attempted to produce an introduction to the archaeology of Cork city and harbour, and I hope that my choice of sites for inclusion in it will be considered a judicious one. Full details of every archaeological site within the harbour area will become available in the East Cork volume of the Cork Archaeological Survey which, at the time of writing, is in the press. This volume will also include detailed distribution maps of all of these sites, and in view of this I have declined to double-up on the excellent work of the Cork Survey by re-producing similar maps within the present book.

Illustration credits

Fig.2 after P.C.Woodman 1984 (see Further Reading section); figs. 3, 4, 7, 9, 10, 11, 12, 13, 14, 15, 17, 18, 33, 34, 37, 38, 39 and 40 courtesy of the National Museum of Ireland; figs. 5 and 6 after M.J. O'Kelly 1945; figs. 8 and 41 courtesy of Ashmolean Museum, Oxford; figs. 16, 22, 23, 47, 48, 49 and 51 courtesy Cork Public Museum; figs. 18, 19, 24, 29, 53, 54, 57, 58, 59, 60, 61, 62, 64, 65 and 66 courtesy Cork Archaeological Survey; fig. 21 after M.J. O' Kelly 1954; figs. 27 and 28 courtesy of Anne-Marie Lennon; fig. 35 after O'Kelly 1955; fig.36 after Murphy 1961; figs. 44 and 45 courtesy of Maurice Hurley; figs. 46 and 50 courtesy of Dr. Elizabeth Shee-Twohig, Department of Archaeology, University College Cork; figs. 55, 56, 67, 69 (by Kevin Dwyer), 68 (based on drawing by Michael Rice), 70 and 85 courtesy Cork County Council; figs. 71, 72, 73, 75, 79, 80, 81, 82, 83, 84, 86, 87, 88, 89, 90 and 91 courtesy the Royal Irish Academy; fig 74 courtesy Birmingham Central Library, Boulton & Watt Collection.

ONE

The Harbour in the Prehistoric Period

On present evidence the Cork harbour area has been continuously occupied from the later mesolithic or middle stone age period onwards. Indeed, rising sea levels and coastal erosion are likely to have destroyed even earlier mesolithic settlements along the south-east coast of Ireland, and possibly within the harbour area itself. During the mesolithic period small bands of hunter-gatherers, known to us within our area of interest only through surviving scatters of their stone tools, are likely to have fished for salmon in the estuary of the River Lee and to have followed shoals of sea fish along the south-east coast. These small, roaming communities were gradually replaced by new colonists- the first Irish farmers-who had an enormous impact on the local environment by clearing forests for agriculture. But while neolithic aretfacts have been found throughout the harbour area no settlements of this period have yet been discovered within our area of interest.

Standing stones, cremated burials, *fulachta fiadha* (ancient cooking places) and an impressive variety of copper, bronze and gold artefacts all attest to the activities of Bronze Age communities within the harbour area during the period 2500-600 BC. The recent discovery and excavation of a Bronze Age house on Fota Island is a valuable addition to our knowledge of Bronze Age settlement in an area which, by this period, may have already been becoming a gateway for seaborne traffic from the rest of Europe. Iron Age settlement around the harbour, however, is very much a grey area. The Cork helmet horns, which were discovered at the beginning of the present century, are the only Iron Age find of note within the harbour area. These latter are, nonetheless, of both national and international importance, being generally regarded as one of the highpoints of Irish La Tène Iron Age art. Trading contacts between the Iron Age communities of the harbour area and the Roman world were already underway by at least the third century A.D. Contacts such as these were to prepare the way for the introduction of Christianity into Ireland, a development which eventually permeated all levels of ancient Irish society.

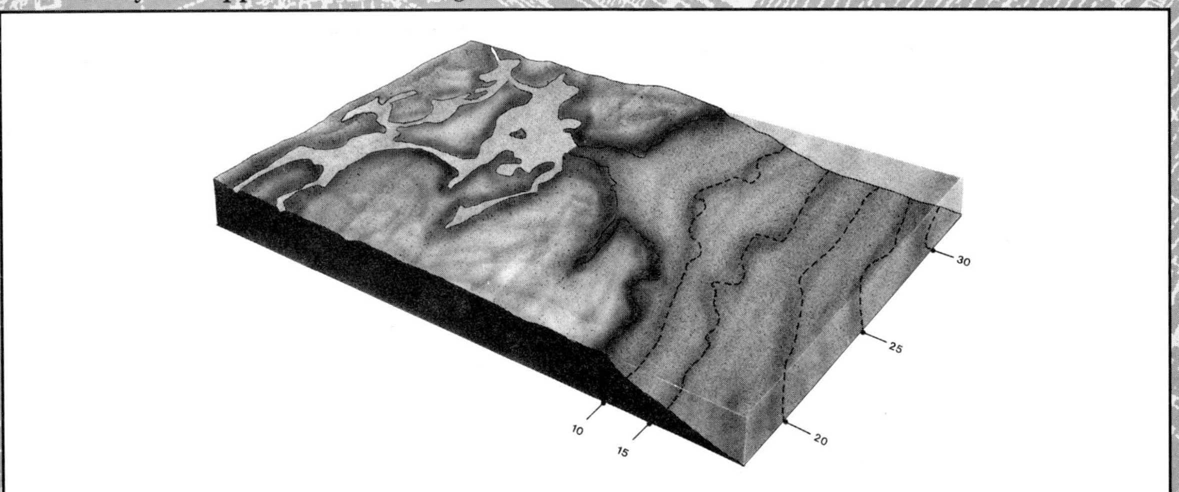

1. Submerged coastline around Cork harbour, depths given in fathoms.

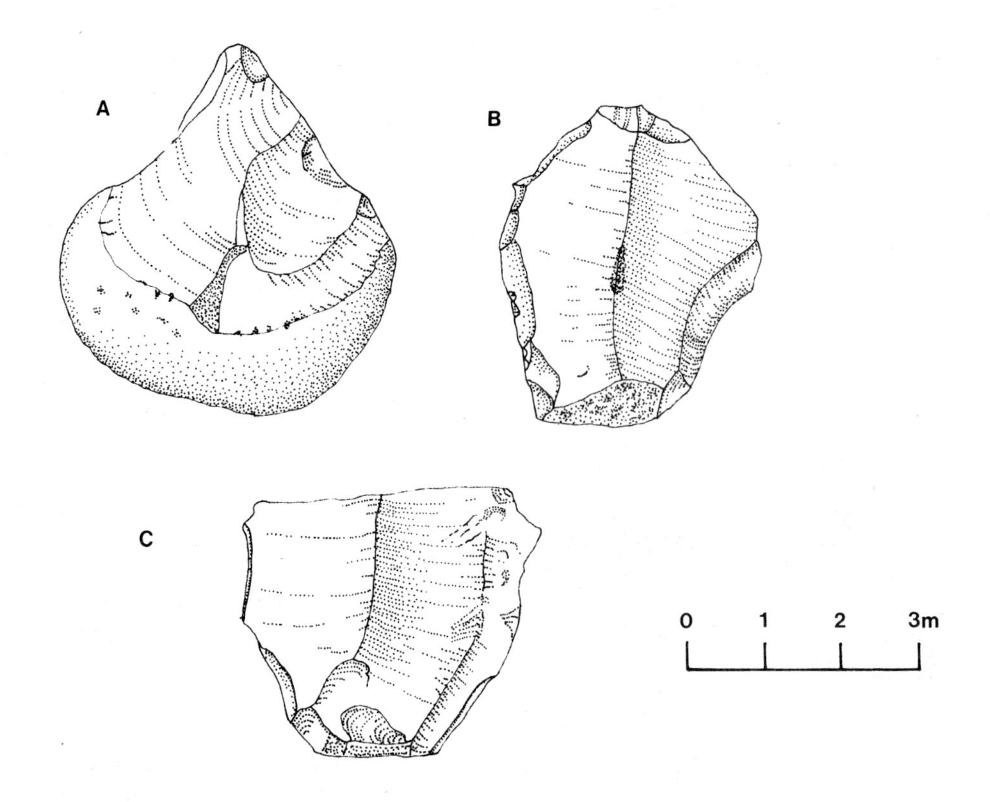

2. "Bann" flakes from Cork harbour area, A and B from Inch, Co. Cork, C from Gyleen, Co. Cork.

THE MESOLITHIC PERIOD: CORK'S EARLIEST SETTLERS

The physical appearance of the harbour has experienced many changes over the last 9,000 years, for around 7,000 BC the sea level around the harbour was at least 30 metres lower than it is today. Lough Mahon in the upper harbour, along with large areas of the lower harbour, would have been a patchwork of marshes, with Great Island rising almost majestically above them. The higher ground bounding the valley of the River Lee would have been covered with Scots pine, whilst hazel scrub and willow trees would have thrived on the valley floor: all in all a remarkable difference from the present day lie of the land. But about 10,000 years ago the ice sheets, which covered vast expanses of land and sea around Europe and North America, began to melt as temperatures gradually began to rise. The melt water from the ice eventually ran off into the seas, and areas of what was then dry land became encroached upon by rising sea levels.

Some of the ice sheets which had covered Ireland were up to 350m thick, and the cumulative effect of this almost imcomprehensible weight on the land mass covered by it was to compress it. When this weight was removed by the melt water the land was allowed to spring up again, and in the north of Ireland the level of the land rose faster then the rise in sea level, creating what are called raised beaches, which in some cases are about 8m above present-day sea level. Large areas of Munster were not covered by ice during the Pleistocene, and up until quite recently it seemed that enormous areas of land on the south coast of Ireland were lost to the rising sea. There can be little doubt that some areas of land are likely to have been submerged in this fashion, but the full picture now appears to have been quite different. For it is now known that that sea level in the Cork harbour area around 7500 years ago was only 12m lower than it is today, and so it is unlikely that large areas of land were flooded by the sea.

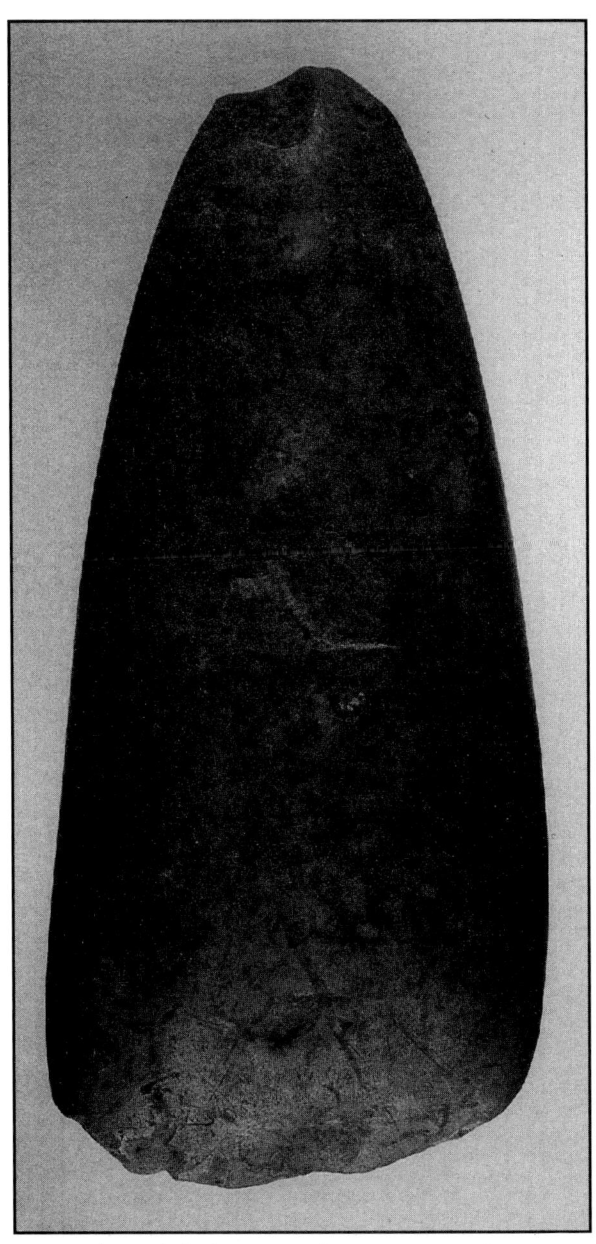

3. *Neolithic polished stone axe from Ravenswood near Carrigaline, Co. Cork, discovered in 1863. 15.5cm long,3cm thick.*

The first people to settle in the harbour area belong to the *mesolithic* or middle stone age. They lived by hunting, fishing, collecting shellfish and gathering nuts and berries, and produced a distinctive range of stone tools. Early mesolithic people, who lived in the period 7000-5500 BC, manufactured small, finely made stone tools of either flint or chert called *microliths*. But thus far sites of this period in County Cork have only been found in the valley of the River Blackwater. Indeed, most early mesolithic sites in the greater harbour area are likely to have either been submerged beneath the rising seas or destroyed by coastal erosion.

The earliest evidence for human settlement within the harbour area dates to the later mesolithic period (5500-3500 BC). Later mesolithic stone tools are generally larger than those of the early mesolithic, and typical of these is the so-called "Bann flake". These are named after the area around the River Bann in Northern Ireland where many similar early prehistoric flint tools have been found. At least three Bann flakes have been found within the harbour area, two near Gyleen on the eastern side of the harbour and a further example on Fota Island. Other flint tools from the Gyleen area may also date to the later mesolithic period, and may well have been associated with a settlement site of this period. A further harbour site at Dunpower, at which later mesolithic implements were found, may well have been a prime site for any later mesolithic fishing community. Communities such as these would have followed shoals of sea fish along the coast of Cork, and may also, perhaps, have hunted boar in the forests on higher ground.

THE NEOLITHIC PERIOD

Colonies of farmers had become established in Ireland by around 4000 BC, in the period called the *neolithic* or new stone age. Ireland's earliest farmers introduced the first domesticated animals – cattle, sheep, pig and goat – to these shores, along with domesticated plants such as emmer, wheat and barley. Their way of life contrasted sharply with that of the preceeding mesolithic period, during which bands of hunter-gatherers had moved from site to site in accordance with the seasons. As herds of animals and crops needed to be tended all year round, settled communities in more or less permanent locations became established. The "tool kit" of the Neolithic farmer was also quite different to that of the mesolithic hunter-gatherer. Polished stone axes were in use in the mesolithic period, but as these made short work of virgin forest, they would have been an important everyday item in the neolithic household. In many areas farming could not have been undertaken until such time as virgin forest had been cut down. The harvesting and general processing of crops, however, required new implements: flint sickles for cutting the stalks of cereal crops and primitive quern stones for reducing the cereal grains to coarse meal or flour. But perhaps the most important aspect of neolithic technology was the ability to manufacture pottery vessels which, in addition to being important aids in cooking and baking, would also have been used as storage vessels.

NEOLITHIC ARTEFACTS IN THE HARBOUR AREA

At least six neolithic polished stone axes have been found in the harbour area, two from the Carrigaline area, three from the Mahon peninsula and one from Ballinaspig Mor (western city suburbs). After a preliminary shaping or "roughing-out", these are likely to have been laboriously ground down by continual rubbing against a wetted sandstone grinding block. Great care was usually taken to ensure that all surfaces of the axe were highly polished, and in many cases an extra gloss may have been imparted to the axe with a leather cloth. The axe would then have been slotted into a wooden haft or handle to enable the person wielding it to get the full weight of their body behind the swing. All in all, the manufacture of one of these axes could have taken an entire day. A small number of neolithic flint tools, which included a leaf- shaped arrowhead and some scrapers, have also come to light in the Carrigtohill area.

4. Neolithic polished stone axe from Carrigaline area.

There are no excavated neolithic settlements within the harbour area, but we should not be too put out by this. Up until very recently it was thought that most areas of Munster remained unpopulated until the neolithic period. Certain areas, indeed, were thought not to have been occupied until the Bronze Age. Since the 1980s, however, our knowledge of the early prehistory of southern Munster has advanced in leaps and bounds. We now know that parts of counties Waterford, Cork and Kerry had been colonised by at least the early mesolithic period, and there is every expectation that further mesolithic sites will be found. The neolithic period, on the other hand, is generally seen as an era of expanding settlement. And as archaeologists have often taken the existence of megalithic tombs as a sign of neolithic settlement, their absence from a particular area often led to the conclusion that the area concerned was not occupied by neolithic communities. Irish neolithic burials did not always involve the construction of impressive megalithic tombs, and so we cannot rule out the possibility that areas without such tombs were not colonised during the neolithic period. This applies to the greater part of the harbour area, but as we shall now see there are in fact two megalithic structures on the eastern side of the harbour.

MEGALITHIC TOMBS

The megalithic tomb at Castlemary near Cloyne would have originally been much larger. It appears to have been covered with an earthen mound, and it seems that some of the large stones which would have defined its side walls have been removed. Opinion is divided as to what type of megalithic structure it represents. The Ordnance Survey's Megalithic Survey has declined to include it in its official lists, but it has also been suggested that it was part of a wedge tomb. Such tombs are generally "wedge-shaped", tapering outwards from their narrower eastern ends in the direction of their wider (and generally higher) western ends. They have a central aisle or gallery covered over with large roofing slabs, whilst a large stone slab at the western end was often used to prevent access into the main burial chamber. There is a marked concentration of wedge tombs in the western part of the county Cork, which noticeably thins out towards the east. If the Castlemary megalith was a wedge tomb (and there is no certainty about this) then it could possibly date to the late neolithic/Early Bronze Age period (c.3000-2500 BC).

The megalithic tomb at Rostellan has also been excluded from the Megalithic Survey's official lists. It consists of three upright stones and a capstone, which had at one time fallen down but was later repositioned. The Rostellan "dolmen" is similar in certain respects to Irish neolithic portal tombs, but not enough to be confidently identified as such. Rostellan remains somewhat enigmatic, though its location has in the past been cited as evidence for rising sea levels during the neolithic period. The site is flooded at high tide and it has been assumed that this was not the intention of its original builders. Some have argued that in the period in which the megalith was built, the site chosen by its builders would have been well away from the foreshore. As it is now partly flooded at high tide, it has been assumed that in the period since it was built sea level in the harbour area has risen.

THE BRONZE AGE

THE EARLY BRONZE AGE (2500-1500 BC).

Towards the end of the neolithic period a new and distinctive type of pottery vessel called a

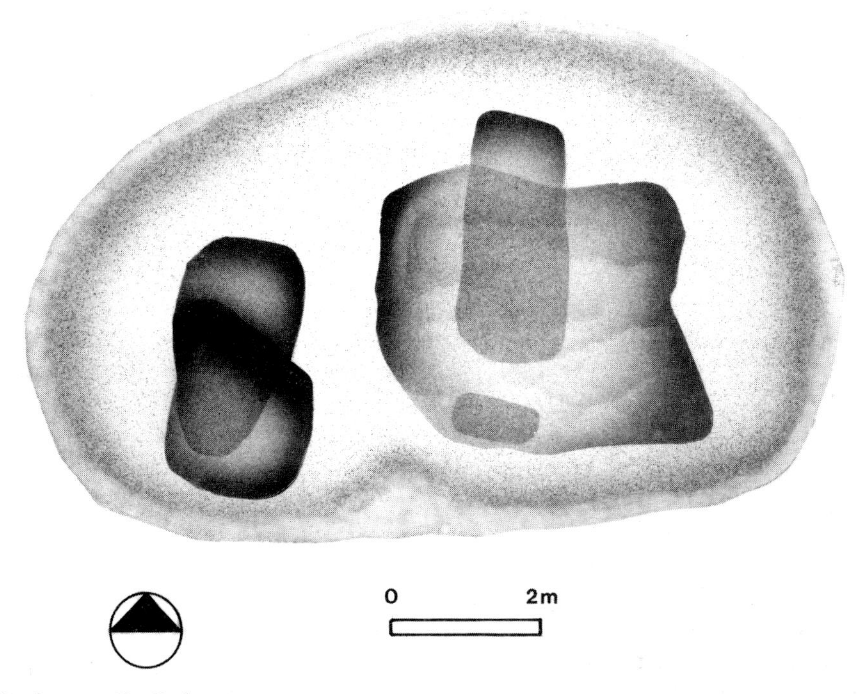

5. Megalith at Castlemary, Co. Cork.

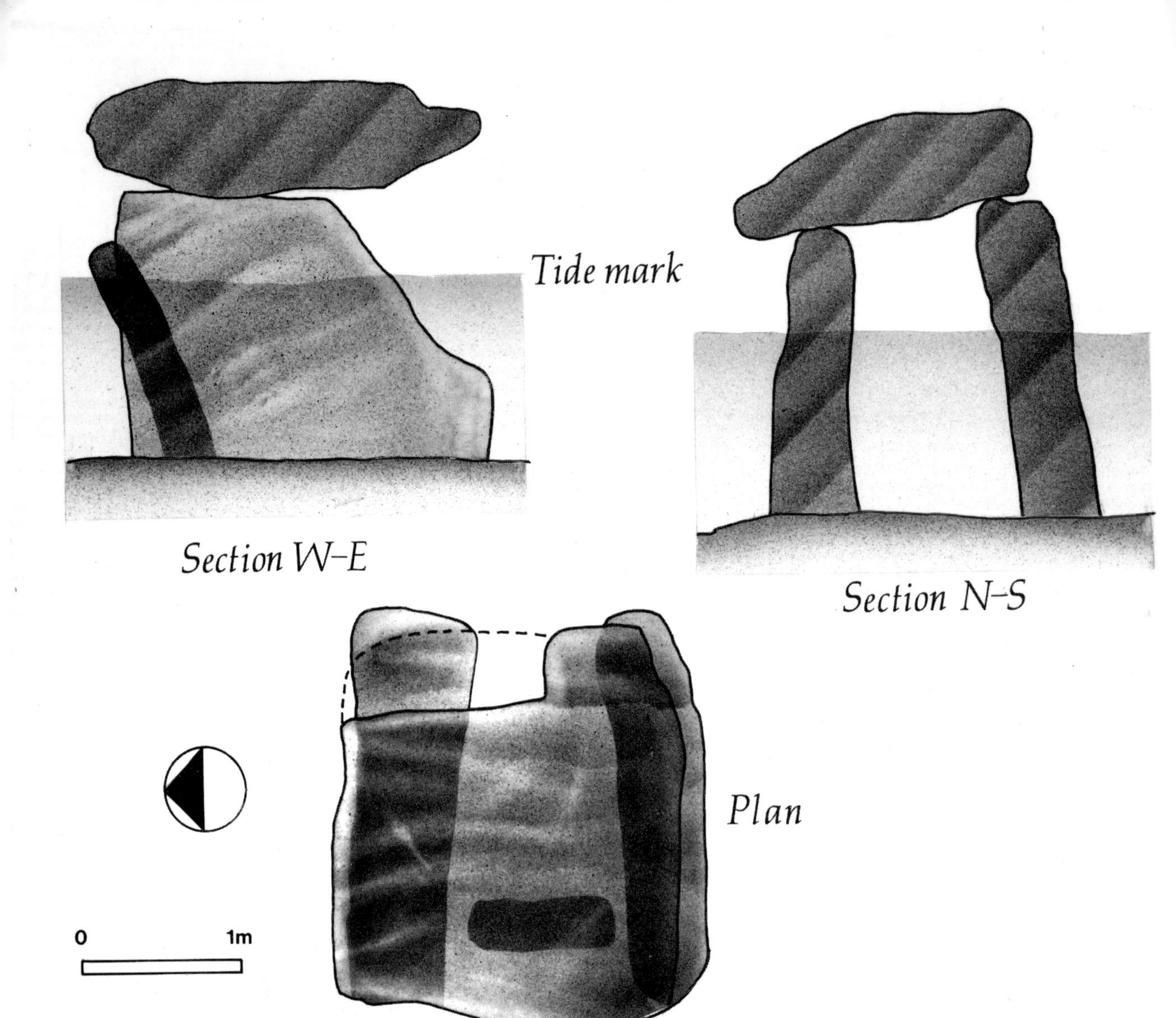

6. Rostellan "dolmen", Co. Cork.

beaker (because of its resemblance to a beaker or tumbler) was introduced into Ireland. It occurs in various forms, and more often than not it is found deposited with items such as flint arrowheads and archers' wristguards in "beaker" graves. The most important feature of many beaker burials, however, is that they contain the earliest metal objects to have been discovered in Ireland.

Whereas the introduction of farming into Ireland is associated with the arrival of new people, the earliest metalworking activity on this island appears to have been brought about through trading and cultural contacts. Indeed, most archaeologists are now at pains to stress that "beaker" is a style of pottery rather than a "people", whereas it was once common to speak of "Beaker folk". It is now generally accepted that the whole beaker phenomenon did not involve an influx of new settlers, but rather that "beaker" items were exchanged and widely imitated throughout Europe.

The earliest Irish metal artefacts were made from either copper or gold. Mount Gabriel, near Schull in west Cork, was one of the most important sources of copper in prehistoric Ireland. It is perhaps because of this that the flat copper axes of the Early Bronze Age have turned up more frequently in the general Munster area than anywhere else in Ireland. These early copper axes, which are often quite primitive, were cast in open stone moulds. At least one exam-

7. *Flat copper axe-head from Carrigaline, Co. Cork. 14cm long, 0.8cm thick.*

8. Gold lunula from near Midleton, Co. Cork, found with two or three others in 1867. (Courtesy Ashmolean Museum, Oxford)

ple of a flat copper axe has been found in the harbour area, in the townland of Carrigaline West.

Amongst the early gold objects found within the harbour area are a series of small, decorated gold discs, and at least two crescent-shaped gold collars called *lunulae*. There are two gold discs from Cloyne and one from Castletreasure near Douglas, each of which are decorated with wheel and cross motifs. Hammered sheet gold was used in their manufacture, and the decoration (as in all of the other known examples), was worked up in relief from the obverse face. The technique involved is called *repoussé,* and the craftsman would have used a small punch to produce the desired effect. It is widely believed that these discs were sewn onto clothes as ornaments, with perhaps the holes punched through the centre enabling them to serve as ornamental buttons or pendants. In this regard the Castletreasure disc is particularly interesting, because its outer edges have clearly been nicked by stitches. Unfortunately, little else is known about the twenty or so discs of this type which have been found in Ireland, but on present evidence they would appear to date to the Beaker and Early Bronze Age periods.

Two, and possibly three, lunulae were discovered in a field near Midleton in 1867. Only two of these can definitely be said to have been associated with this find, and of these one is in the Ashmolean Museum in Oxford: the whereabouts of the second Midleton lunula are presently unknown. There is also a third lunula in the Ashmolean collections which may have been found with the other two in 1867, but there can be no certainty about this. The Midleton lunulae are of what has been called the "classical" type, a term which has been given to the most sophisticated examples.

9. Prehistoric (?) amber beads, Carrigaline area, Co. Cork.

10. Prehistoric (?) amber ball, Carrigaline area, Co. Cork.

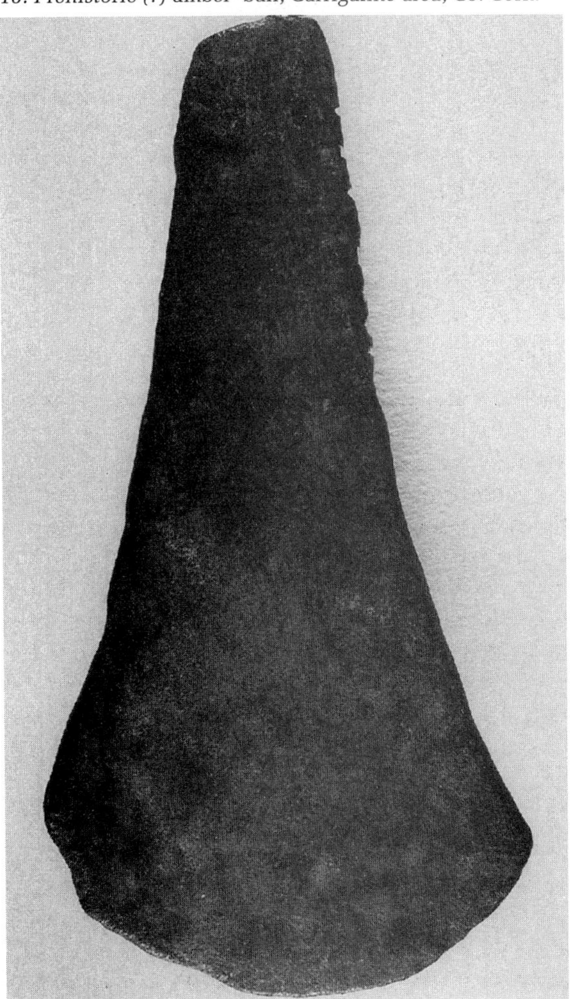

11. Flat bronze axe-head from Ballinure, Mahon peninsula, 9.1cm long, 4.9cm wide.

12. Bronze, flanged axe with stop-ridge, Carrigaline area, Co. Cork. 10.5cm long, 4.5cm wide across cutting edge.

Classical lunulae, which are very rare outside Ireland, were clearly the work of master goldsmiths. They also contain more gold than the other known varieties, which was skilfully beaten into much thinner sheets. It has also been noticed that their extremely fine and precise decoration is very similar to that found on Beaker objects, and because of this some archaeologists believe that they date to the late Beaker period. However, gold was by no means the only material used for ornaments. There are at least three amber beads and a curious amber ball from the harbour area, which may be of Bronze Age date. Amber necklaces of this period have been found elsewhere in Ireland, and it seems likely that the amber itself was imported from Scandinavia.

Bronze is an alloy of copper and tin, but while copper existed in abundance in south western County Cork, tin would have to have been imported. The nearest and most likely source for this was Cornwall. Flat open moulds were also used for the earliest bronze axes, but with a type of mould designed to give the axe a wider cutting edge. After the molten metal had cooled down the axe would then be finished by a bronze smith, who hammered it into shape and later ground and polished it. At least two examples of such axes have been found within the immediate environs of the city, which include a small flat axehead from Ballinure.

THE MIDDLE BRONZE AGE (1500-1200 B.C.)

The next important developments in the design of axes were geared towards improving the way in which their handles were attached. The sides of the axe now began to be hammered up into flanges, which gave an improved type of L-shaped handle an added grip to the body of the axe. Flanged axes began to appear in the Early Bronze Age, but at a slightly later period a ridge was added to the flat face of the axehead to stop the haft or handle from slipping. A good example of a flanged axe with a "stop ridge" has turned up in the Carrigaline area. The introduction of the palstave, however, in which the flanges and the stop ridge of the axe were formed in a single piece, was one of the more notable improvements associated with Middle Bronze Age metalworking. This arrangement provided a firmer grip for the haft, and the addition of a loop cast on the side of the axe (as on an axe found in Carrigaline West) helped to fasten the leather thong used to tie the axe to the haft. It is difficult to say which of these axes would have been used in warfare. Indeed some of them may well have been multi-purpose tools, being used to cleave wood or flesh as the occasion arose. Only a handful of bronze age weapons have been found in the harbour area, and only one of these can be associated with the Middle Bronze Age. This is a spearhead from Carrigaline with cast side loops, which were used to bind it to the shaft of the spear. The main body of the spearhead also has a socket which could be slotted on to the spear's shaft.

THE LATE BRONZE AGE (1200-600 B.C.)

In the preceding period two-piece stone moulds had been used to create more elaborate cast bronze work such as the socketed spearheads. But in the Later Bronze Age clay was used for moulds, where the shape of the piece to be cast was carved in wood and then impressed into the clay. The characteristic socketed axes with side loops of the Later Bronze Age were manufactured in this fashion, and at least five of these have been found in the Cork harbour area.

Sometime around the beginning of the first millenium B.C. swords were introduced into Ireland. Earlier dirks and rapiers were no more than glorified daggers, and the first Irish swords were a considerable improvement on these. The rapier could only be used for thrusting but the sword, with its extended hilt and greater overall length, provided not only a firmer grip but could be used as a slashing weapon. The handle itself, which would have been of either bone or wood, was held in place by bronze rivets. Three bronze age swords have been found in the harbour area, two of which were found near the city; the third being recovered in the Carrigaline area.

13. Bronze spearhead with cast side loops from Ravenswood near Carrigaline, Co. Cork. 11.5cm long.

14. *Late Bronze Age socketed axehead from Kilbarry, Co. Cork, on outskirts of Cork City, discovered in 1849. 8.6cm long.*

BURIALS

To-date only two Bronze Age burials have come to light in the harbour area, one of which dates to the Early Bronze Age period. This was discovered at Oatencake just outside Midleton and contained a small funerary urn, with the cremated remains of a fully grown adult (possibly female), of slender build. The urn itself is of the *cordoned* type, so-called because the decoration is applied in cordons around the upper part of the urn. The Oatencake example was found lying on its side, but normally these urns would be deliberately placed upside down in either a specially dug pit or a slab-lined grave called a cist. Urn burials in pits and cists are characteristic Early Bronze Age burial practices.

In the early 1930s a hilltop cairn 15m in diameter and defined by a kerb of stones was excavated at Curraghbinny. No human remains came to light, but a small mound of stones and clay near the centre of the cairn may well have originally covered an unburnt Bronze Age burial. The stone and clay pile was covered with a spread of charcoal and the bones and teeth of cow. Two deposits of water-smoothened pebbles and a badly preserved bronze ring were also found within the cairn.

The practice of erecting single, upright, standing stones as either boundary or grave

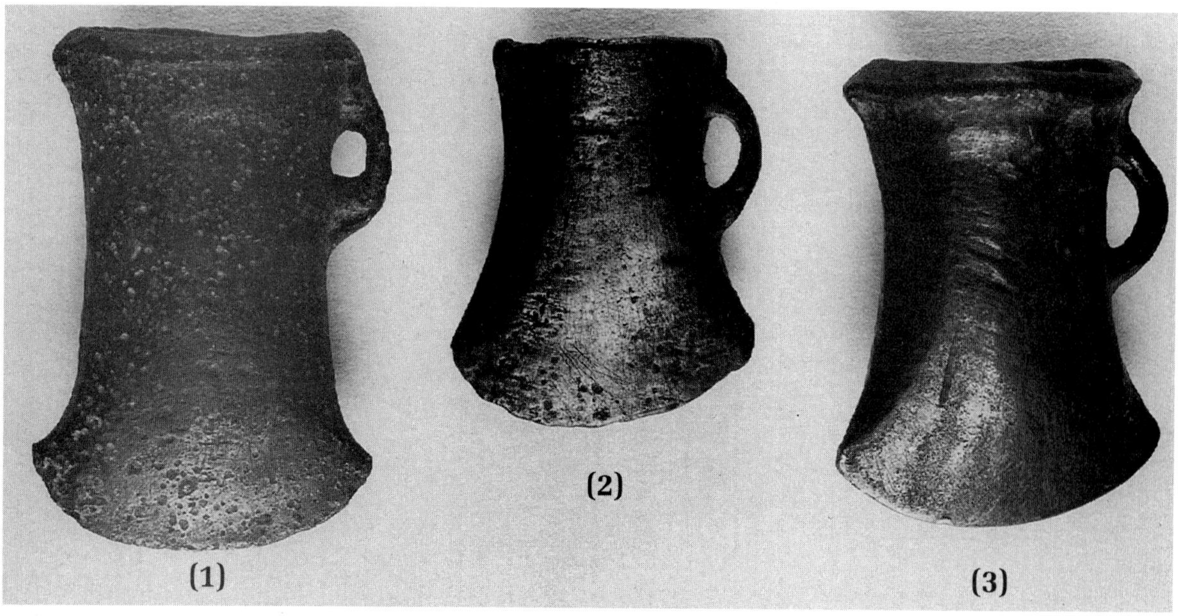

15. *Three bronze socketed axeheads from Ravenswood, near Carrigaline, Co. Cork. (1) 6.5cm long, (2) 4.8cm long, (3) 5.5cm long.*

16. Cordoned urn from Oatencake, near Midleton, Co. Cork.

markers appears to have begun in the Early Bronze Age. Indeed, the vast majority of standing stones which have either been excavated or otherwise interfered with in Ireland have had some form of association with either Beaker or Early Bronze Age burials. The Cork Archaeological Survey has located at least 25 standing stones within the harbour area, many of which are still standing. There is a noticeable concentration of these on the high ground to the north of the city in the Gurranbraher and Killeens areas, but these are, relatively speaking, quite small examples. However, relatively tall examples such as the 2.3m high stone at Ballygrissane on the eastern side of the harbour are known. Thus far none of the Cork harbour examples have been excavated.

FULACHTA FIADH

There are almost 2,000 burnt mounds, or *fulachta fiadh* ("cooking places of the fianna") as they are generally referred to in Ireland, in Cork county. They are the most numerous archaeological field monuments in the county, and some 38 examples have been located in the Cork harbour area. In the field they usually take the form of low, kidney or horseshoe-shaped mounds. When excavated these mounds have been found to be made up of fire-shattered stone, charcoal and ash, the residues of a cooking practice which in Ireland has been scientifically dated to the Bronze Age. A pit was first cut near a stream or in a marshy area, and the sides of it were lined with either wooden planks or stone slabs to form a water trough. In most cases the trough would have been filled automatically by water seeping in through its sides, and it is no coincidence that almost half

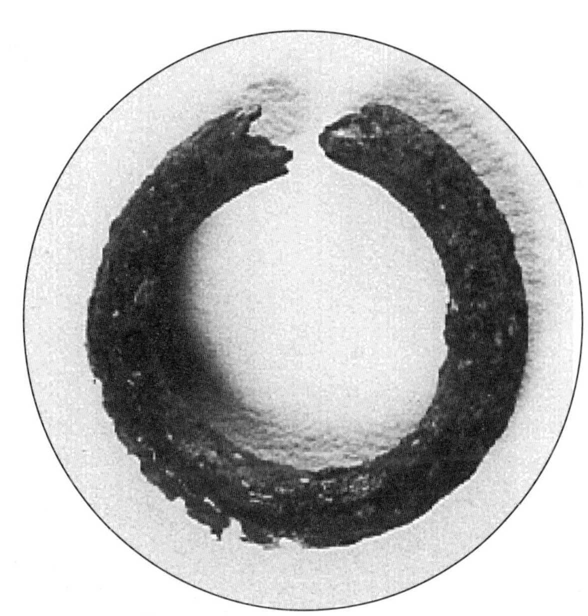

17. Bronze ring from Bronze-Age burial at Curraghbinny, Co. Cork.

19. Standing stone, Gearagh, near Ballynacorra, Co. Cork.

18. Standing stone, Gurranbraher, on the northern edge of the Cork city suburbs.

20. Reconstruction of Killeens fulacht fiadh *trough.*

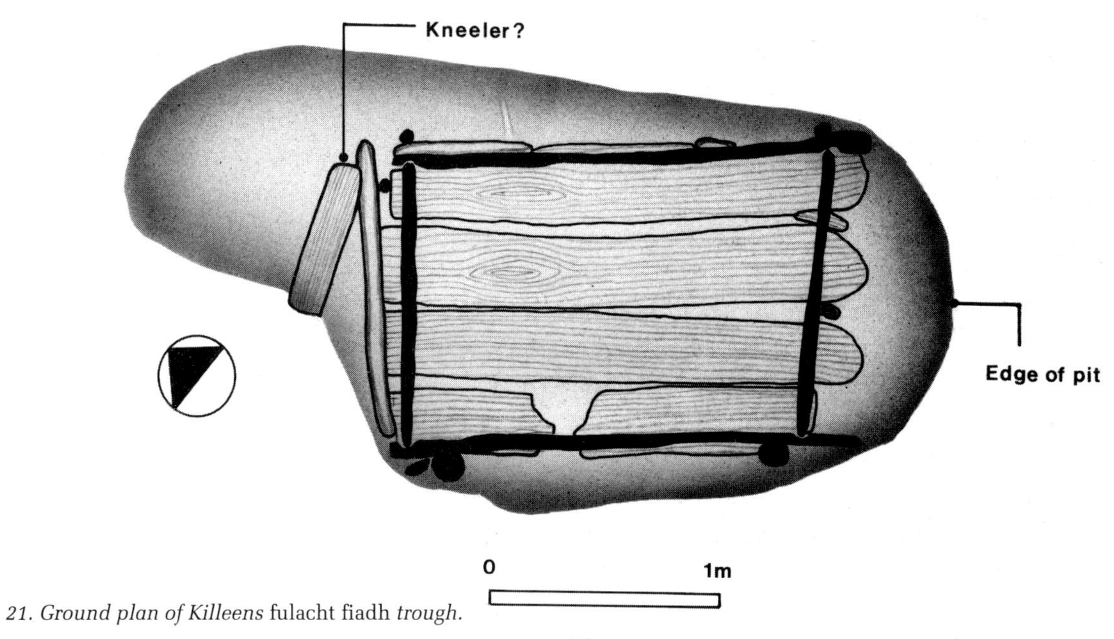

21. Ground plan of Killeens fulacht fiadh *trough.*

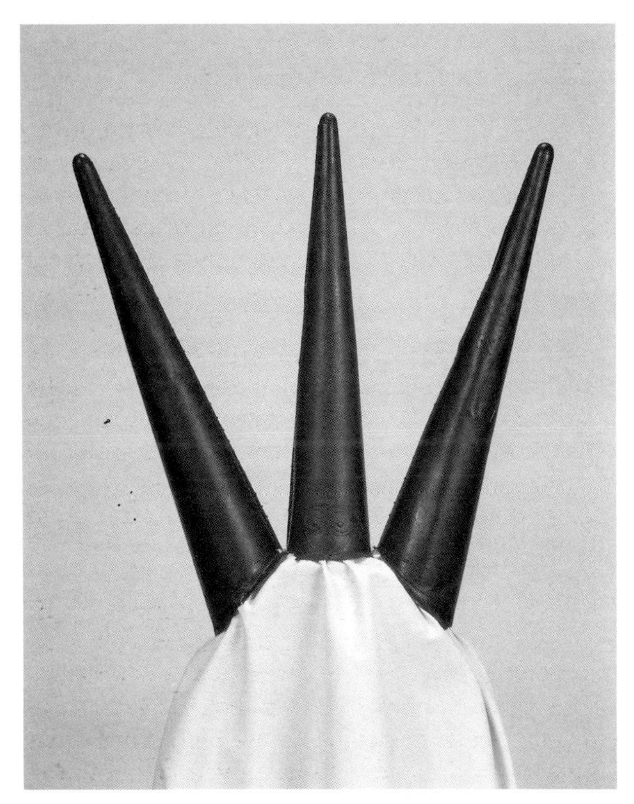

22. The Cork "Helmet" Horns.

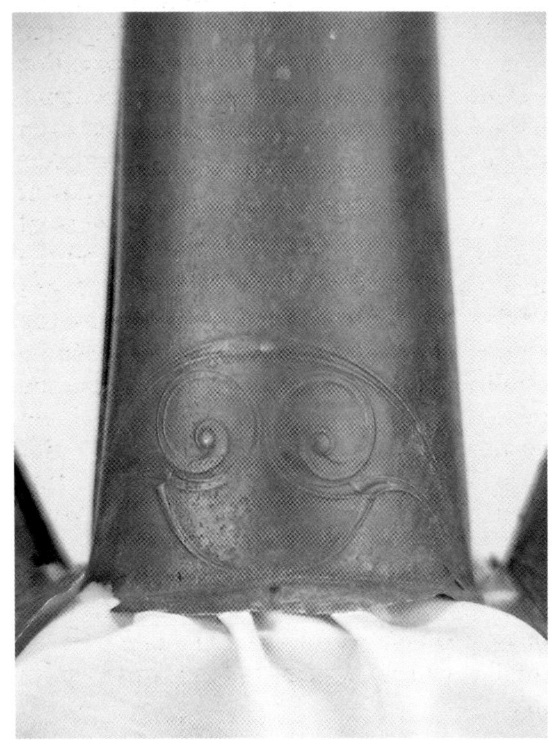

23. Detail of ornament on one of the Cork horns.

of the fulacht fiadha in County Cork were located near streams. Stones were heated in a hearth near the trough, until such time as they became red-hot, whereupon they were tossed into the trough to bring the water in it to the boil. A joint of meat, which may or may not have been wrapped in a jacket of straw, would then have been placed in the water. The water itself was kept at boiling point by the addition of further red-hot stones until such time as the cooking had been completed. Modern experiments with this ancient cooking method indicate that the water in the trough could be brought to the boil in little more than half an hour and that a 4.5kg joint could be cooked throughout in less than four hours. Within the harbour area the most important site of this type to have been exacavated is that at Killeens, just to the north of the city. A plank-lined wooden trough at this site, around 52cm deep, yielded radio carbon dates of 1763 and 1556 bc. A gold-plated copper ring was also recovered from this site, and is one of a handful of artefacts which have come to light during fulacht fiadha excavations in Ireland.

Up until quite recently fulacht fiadha, standing stones and assorted burials have provided the only real clues regarding human settlement in the harbour area during the Bronze Age. But in 1992 a possible late neolithic/Early Bronze Age habitation site was excavated on Fota Island, the principal feature of which was an oval, post-built building 8 x 4m in extent, which had a small "porch" at its entrance similar to a Bronze Age house site at Ballyveelish in County Tipperary. The finds from the Fota Island site included flints and some prehistoric pottery, and the discovery of the site has raised hopes of similar discoveries not only on the island but within the greater harbour area.

THE IRON AGE

The first use of iron objects in Ireland is currently believed to date to around 500 BC, but shortly before this period bronze swords were in use which appear to be copies of iron types associated with the Halstatt or early European Iron Age. Indeed, iron artefacts of the Halstatt type are poorly represented in Ireland, and while those of the later La Tène Iron Age are commoner very little is known about their dating. All in all the Iron Age is very much a grey area where Ireland is concerned, and the same state of affairs extends to the Cork Harbour area, with a single exception. In 1909, near the south jetties in the Victoria Road area, three remarkable bronze cones were accidentally discovered. The "Cork horns", as they became known, appear to have formed part of some form of leather headgear, but for archaeologists the most interesting feature of these "horns" is the way in which they were decorated. The designs fashioned on the Cork horns bear a strong resemblance to those of two other Iron age artefacts, the Bann disc, which was recovered from the River Bann near Loughan Island, and the Petrie Crown, the find-spot of which is not known. Indeed, so similar are the designs on all three of these objects that they may well have been made by the same craftsman. The Cork horns, the Bann disc and the Petrie crown have recently been described as the high point of La Tène art in Ireland, and have been dated to the first century A.D.

Ireland had never featured prominently in the colonial ambitions of the Roman empire. Nonetheless, it is quite clear that mariners from Roman Britain were familiar with the coastline of Ireland. The Roman material which has come to light in Ireland appears to have been the result of trade with Roman Britain, contacts which ultimately led to the introduction of Christianity into Ireland. Clear-cut evidence of contact between the Cork harbour area and the Roman empire in the early centuries A.D. has been found at Cuskinny, which faces the entrance to the harbour. In the late 1890s a hoard of Roman coins, ranging in date from the reigns of Claudius Gothicus (A.D. 278-270) and the younger Constantine (A.D.337), along with coins of other emperors such as Constantius Chlorus and Constantine the Great, were unearthed here. There can be little doubt that trade and other cultural contacts existed between the Iron Age Irish tribes and the contemporary Roman world, the effect of which, as we shall now see, brought Ireland into a wider world.

TWO

The Early Medieval Period

The early medieval period in Ireland is generally taken to be that between the 5th and the 12th centuries A.D. It begins with the first Christian missions and ends (somewhat artificially) with the beginning of the Anglo-Norman settlement. For the first time Ireland enters history through the eyes of its own inhabitants.

Ireland never became part of the Roman empire, although it was neither isolated from, nor immune to, Roman influences. The presence of Roman artefacts in Ireland can in part be explained by Irish raids on the Roman province of Brittania, though it is also clear that traders from Roman Britain are also likely to have made the short sea journey to Ireland. Some of the Roman material in Ireland is increasingly being viewed by Irish archaeologists as the products of trade with Roman Britain. As early as the 1st century A.D. the Roman historian Tacitus could confidently assert that "through commercial intercourse and the merchants there is a better knowledge of the harbours and approaches [of Ireland]." In the same account we are told that the interior of Ireland was "little known", but the likelihood is that before the withdrawal of the Roman garrison from Britain in A.D. 406, that Roman traders had already penetrated inland. From the co-ordinates provided by the second century A.D. Greek geographer Claudius Ptolemaius (Ptolemy), it is clear that the relative positions of the major Irish rivers such as the Shannon (Senos) and the Boyne (Buvinda) were known to him. The exact source of his information is unknown, but the degree of accuracy involved would suggest that this may have been common knowledge.

On the south-east coast the River Dabrona is indicated, roughly where we would expect the River Lee to be, and it has been suggested that these were one and the same. Dabrona, it has been argued, is a medieval copyist's error for Sabrona, later Sabhrann, the earliest known Irish name for the River Lee. If we assume that this was the case it follows that the approaches to Cork harbour were known, if not to all of the mariners of the Mediterranean, then at least to those of Roman Britain. Cork harbour is likely to have been the entry point for most of the exotic goods found at a number of early medieval settlement sites in the greater Cork area. The likelihood is that this post-Roman trade with Britain and the Mediterranean was a continuation of earlier trading links.

The introduction of Christianity drew Ireland into a wider, though in many ways, alien world. The trappings of Roman rule - towns, currency, public works, organised communications and a literate bureaucracy - did not exist in Ireland. But the keynote of early Irish Christianity was its flexibility, and within a few centuries the new religion had ingrained itself upon a non-urban, tribal society. Yet there were some compromises which could not be made. For Christianity is also a written message, and Irish clerics had to be able to read Latin, the language of the Roman world and, after its demise, the official language of the Roman Church. Their mastery of this and the eventual writing down of their own language enabled Irish clerics to enter the mainstream of early medieval European culture.

24. Modern agriculture and the early medieval landscape: aerial view of partly destroyed ringfort at Ballynatra, Co. Cork.

EARLY MEDIEVAL SETTLEMENT AROUND CORK HARBOUR

The most common and distinctive form of early medieval settlement site around the harbour is the ringfort. This is usually a circular, ocassionally oval, area surrounded by one or more earthen banks and ditches. But while it is often the case that the enclosing earthworks can be quite imposing, it is clear from the early documentary sources and the location of many sites that these were as much a badge of rank as a deterrent to potential attackers. A large number of sites, for example, are built on slopes which would allow an enemy to command high ground; whilst the entrance (the weakest point) invariably has a simple gateway which any determined enemy could easily breach. Thus many may not have been "forts" in the conventional sense of structures designed to endure sieges although the ringworks, while they could not be entirely relied upon in the event of a raid for livestock, would at least make the aim of the raiders more difficult.

In more recent times they have been known as "fairy forts" and the traditional taboos about interfering with them in the Irish countryside are legion. Many landowners have taken such tales to heart and this, in no small way, has enabled many of these sites to survive. Modern farmers have little time for fireside tales. Raths get in the way of mechanised agriculture and many have been levelled to accommodate it. So one form of ignorance, a tolerance based on the alleged supernatural consequences of enraging the fairies, has been replaced by another form dictated by more profitable farming.

In Irish the terms *rath,* dun and *lios* are used to denote earthen ringworks, whilst *caisel* (from the Latin *castellum,* "fort") is generally used for sites enclosed by stone walls. The term rath is perhaps a more neutral term for these sites, for these were essentially enclosed farmsteads rather than the military installations which the term ringfort seems to suggest. Both the archaeological and documentary evidence leave us with little doubt as to the main uses to which these sites were put: they were the homesteads of the nobility and strong farmers

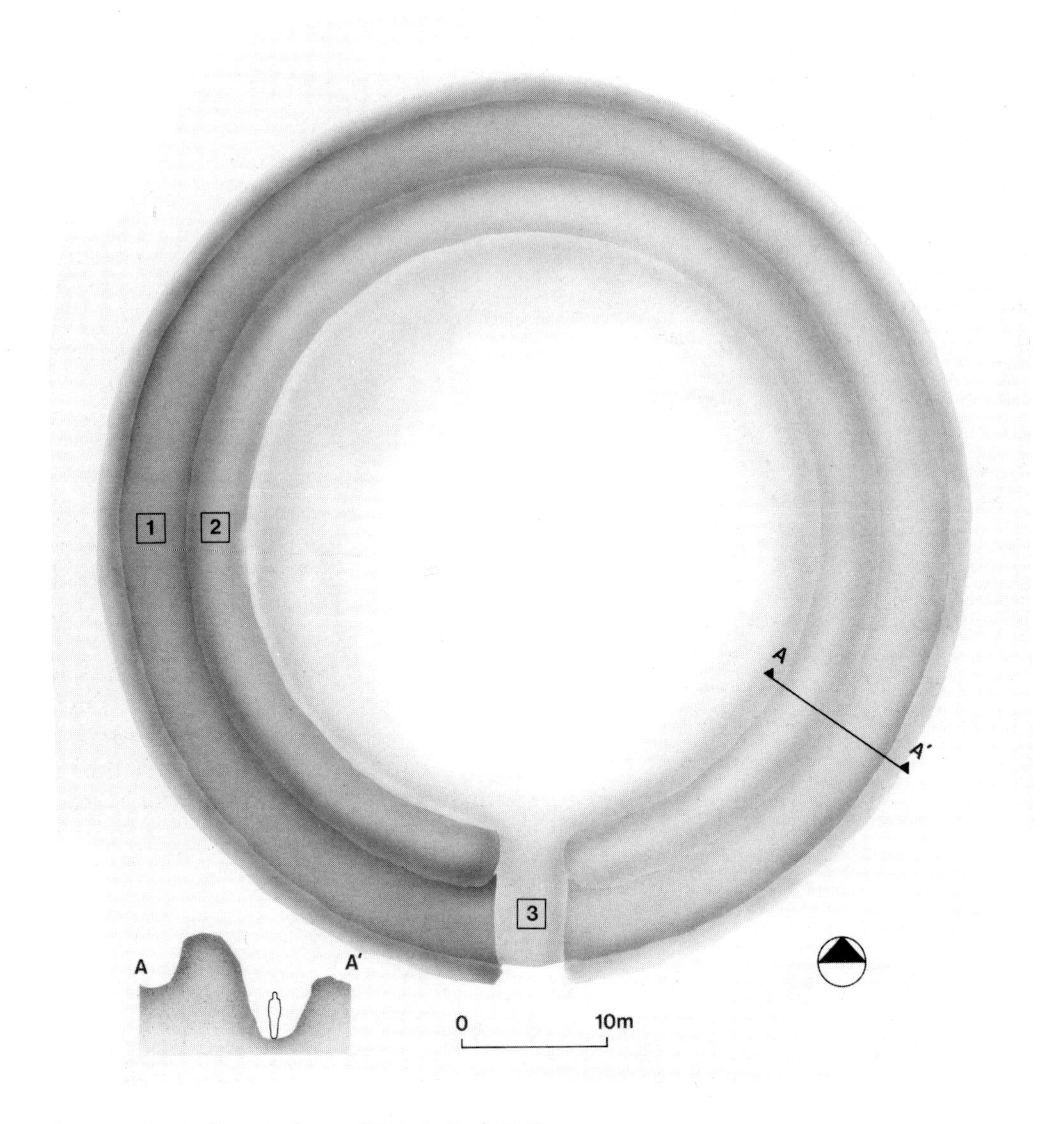

25. Main features of univallate ringfort. ***1.*** *Ditch;* ***2.*** *Bank;* ***3.*** *Causeway.*

and, in certain instances, cattle compounds. As many as 60,000 of these sites may have been built in the early medieval period, although most of these would not have been continuously occupied.

There are no cashels within our area of interest, and in County Cork and elsewhere these are generally found in upland areas where stone is readily available, and where the formation of earthen banks through ditch-digging was virtually impossible. In earthen raths the bank is formed with the material excavated from the ditch, and low stone walls were occasionally built around the inner and outer faces of the bank to hold the upcast earth and rock in place. Bedrock was often encountered during ditch digging, and this was generally broken up and incorporated into the material used in the construction of the bank. In some instances it was used to form a counter-scarp bank on the outer edge of the ditch, the overall effect of which was to give greater depth to the ditch. Raths can have anything from one (univallate) to three (trivallate) banks and ditches, and while there are trivallate sites within the county these are much rarer than those with either one or two (bivallate) sets of concentric earthworks.

The Cork Archaeological Survey through archaeological fieldwork, aerial photography and documentary research, have located about 80 raths within the harbour area. Around 40 of these actually survive in various states of preservation, but only two of the total number of sites have been excavated. The vast majority of these sites have a single bank and ditch which are roughly circular in outline, although at least one site at Ballyregan (situated on top of a knoll) is almost oval. Diameters range from 20m, as at Ballintubrid East, to 74m in the case of one of the Glanturkin raths on the eastern side of the harbour. In most cases, however, the Cork Harbour raths are generally between 30 and 40m in diameter. Surviving banks are anything from 1.2 to 1.5m high, although it should be borne in mind that these would have been denuded over the centuries whilst excavations throughout Ireland have shown that there is a marked tendency for the bank to slump downwards into the ditch. The gradual infilling of the ditch is also assisted by the erosion of its sides through frost action and by tree roots and other vegetation, which causes the sides of the ditch to collapse inwards. Thus the original depth of the ditch often bears no relation to that visible today, and when excavated these can be over 2m deep.

LOCATION OF RINGFORTS

Many of the raths around the harbour are built on hill slopes (usually facing southwards), presumably so as to facilitate drainage, although in some instances the interior is sometimes slightly raised to compensate for this, as at Ardra Beg on the eastern side of the harbour. Almost half of the surviving raths were built at elevations of between 100-200ft (c30.5-70m) above sea level, and most of these are to be found on the eastern side of the harbour. The most low-lying sites - between 50-100ft (c15-30.5m.) above sea level- are concentrated in the north-east of the harbour. Indeed, there is only one harbour site, Gortigrenane, which is over 400ft (c.122m) O.D., and the lesson here is that good farming land then, as today, is generally found at lower altitudes. A small number of raths were also built in locations which enabled them to command imposing views. A good example of this is one of the surviving raths at Ballinluska, from which a commanding view over Myrtleville Bay

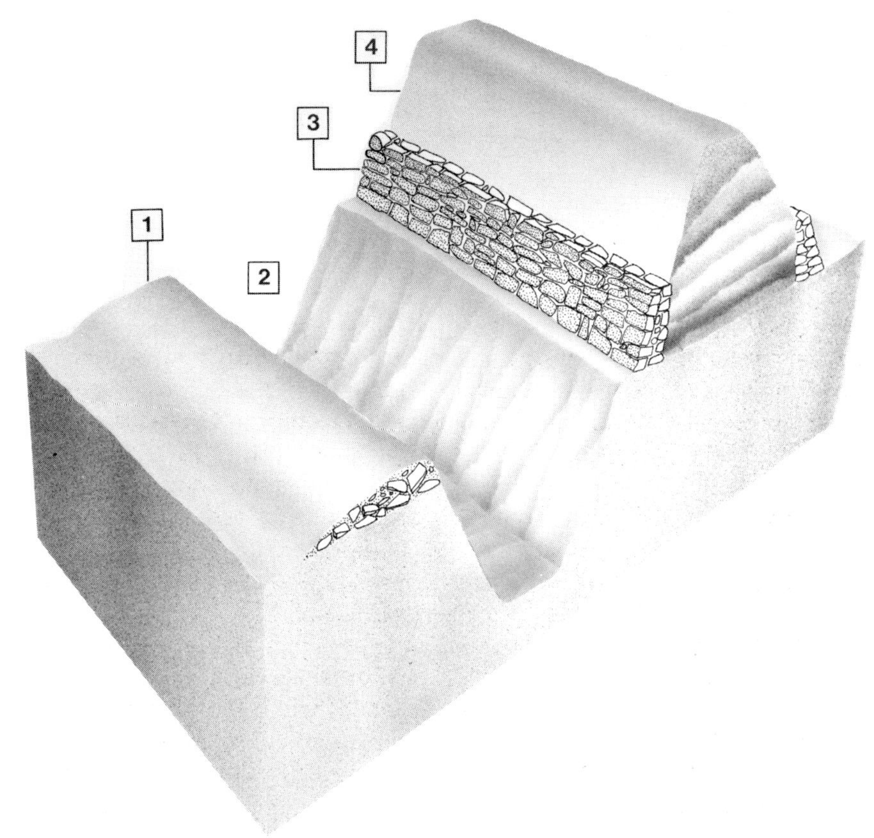

26. Reconstruction of ringfort bank and ditch. ***1.*** *Counter-scarp bank;* ***2.*** *Ditch;* ***3.*** *Revetment wall;* ***4.*** *Bank.*

is at hand from the south-east of the site. The excavated rath at Glanturkin, near Gyleen, occupied a similar position commanding, as it did, good views of the countryside to the south and east, and of Gyleen bay.

With the exception of some five bivallate sites (only three of which survive), all of the Cork harbour raths are univallate. In certain cases, as at the raths at Crosshaven Hill and Trabolgan, sections of stone facing on the earthern banks are still visible, while at Inch, on the eastern side of the harbour, part of a counterscarp bank survives on the north-west of the site. Locating the original entrance to a rath without excavation is often difficult and, indeed, even excavation can sometimes draw a blank. Two of the original three sites at Innygraga have features which may possibly be entrances, but this itself could only be confirmed through excavation. Bivallate raths survive at Trabolgan, Carrigaline and Titeskin, and while on the face of it sites of this type clearly have twice the defences of univallate sites, this is not necessarily an indication of the paranoia of their original inhabitants. The early Irish legal texts suggest that the additional ringworks were more an indication of the social standing of the inhabitants, than of a perceived need on their part for additional defence.

A rath at Ballyshane has a circular enlosure physically linked to it on its south-west side, which may well have been an original feature of it, or which may have been added at a later stage during its occupation. It is well nigh impossible to suggest with certainty what this enclosure was used for. Other sites, while they might not be actually conjoined, may be very close to one another as in the case of two of the Innygraga raths (one of which has been levelled). Yet even if both of these sites were excavated it would still be difficult to establish that both were in use at the same time, and the same is true of all of the surviving raths around the harbour.

SOUTERRAINS

Underground passages known as souterrains are a common feature of Irish raths. They are by no means exclusive to these sites and, indeed,

27. Souterrain at Raheens, near Crosshaven, Co. Cork.

there are examples which do not have any kind of enclosing earthworks. Some of these can often be quite complex, with multiple chambers and interconnecting tunnels, although their original purpose (or purposes) is by no means clear. Certain early medieval Irish texts suggest that they were sometimes used as hiding places by the inhabitants of raths, but there are also indications that they were used for storage. They are often discovered accidentally when, for example, heavy farm machinery causes the roof of a souterrain to collapse. But shallow depressions within a rath or an area which remains dry after heavy rainfall are also tell-tale signs that a souterrain may be present. There were two basic construction techniques used to form these underground passages. The first involved the mining of an underground "cavern" in material solid enough to prevent the tunnels thus formed from caving in or, alterna-

28. Foundation trench of early medieval house excavated at Raheens, Co. Cork

tively, a large construction trench was excavated which was lined with stone walling. In the latter case the chambers and passages were roofed over with large stone slabs, and when this had been completed the entire construction was backfilled. Stone-built air vents leading from one of the passages to the surface are quite common in both earth-cut and stone-walled souterrains.

In 1909 a stone-built souterrain 2.43m long, 1.52m wide and 1.52m high, was discovered on the roadside outside the grounds of Clanricarde House, in the Ballintemple area of the city. It had an entrance shaft 1.21m long, and its side walls had been corbelled (i.e. curved inwards) to support its roofing slabs. An earth-cut souterrain was recently discovered in a suburban garden at Huggart's Land on the southern outskirts of the city, when its roof collapsed. This had a single earth-cut chamber 2.3m by 1.3m and was around 1m high.

EXCAVATED RINGFORTS

Only three Cork harbour ringforts have been excavated, at Glanturkin near Gyleen and two sites in the townland of Raheens near Crosshaven. The Glanturkin site produced no evidence for domestic occupation or material with which it could be dated; and its excavator suggested that it may have served as an animal compound. The Raheens raths (1 and 2), on the other hand, produced clear cut evidence that each had been occupied during the early medieval period. These were 1.5km from the harbour and roughly 400m apart; Raheens 2 being situated to the south-west of Raheens 1. Raheens 1 was 45m in external diameter and was enclosed by two ditches for which, rather curiously, there was no direct evidence for any associated enclosing banks. The inner and outer ditches had U-shaped profiles, the outer ditch being 1.9m deep.

Two circular houses, one with plank side walls (overall diameter 5m), the other constructed with wattling (overall diameter 6m) were excavated in the interior of this rath. But evidence for occupation was not confined to the interior. A series of post sockets and possible storage pits were also investigated outside the rath, although it was not possible to establish whether or not this activity had occurred around the same time as that investigated inside the rath. The perforated hone stone (a sharpening stone with a hole at one end, which may have enabled it to be tied to a belt) and the small iron blade found during the excavation, allow us to assign the broad date "early medieval" to this particular rath. However, the discovery on the same site of early medieval pottery of French origin is a truly remarkable one. For not only does it confirm the provisional dating of this site, it also provides us with important information with regard to the foreign trade of the harbour in this period (see below).

The second Raheens site was a univallate rath 28m in diameter, with a substantial outer ditch 4.3m wide and around 2.1m deep. Excavation confirmed that a break in the enclosing bank, on the south-east of the site, was in fact its original entrance or gateway. The entrance was defined by two large posts, each around 20cm in diameter and set 1m apart, which had a pavement of carefully set pebbles and stone. The excavation of the interior revealed 11 structures, which included at least three round houses, a subrectangular building 6.5m long, and a number of smaller buildings, which may have been outhouses or stores. A stone-walled souterrain, with a single chamber 4m long, was excavated in the south-western section of the site, whilst a construction trench for a further souterrain also came to light. This latter trench appears to have been intended for an unfinished souterrain, the construction of which was abandoned by the occupants of the rath with the trench itself being deliberately filled in. The material used to backfill the trench provided a valuable insight into the diet of the rath's occupants; for along with the bones of cattle and sheep were found oyster, whelk and periwinkle shells. The vertebrae of a whale or a porpoise were also found in this material, the animal itself being either harpooned or washed up on the shoreline of the harbour. Artefacts recovered from the site included a polished stone bead, a hone stone, a couple of perforated stone discs and fragments of shale bracelets, all broadly "early medieval" in date. A further souterrain was discovered accidently outside of the site by earth-moving machinery, when the time available for the excavation had all but ran out. This was a single chambered, drystone structure, which had a creep way leading into a chamber 1.8m beneath the surface.

COASTAL PROMONTARY FORTS

At Dunpower, about one mile east of Power Head, the remains of a coastal promontary fort can be seen on a small headland. Coastal promontary forts may well have their origins in

29. Coastal promontary fort at Dunpower, Co. Cork.

the Iron Age. However, a number of excavated examples such as Dunbeg, Co. Kerry and Dalkey Island, Co. Dublin, were clearly occupied in the early medieval period. They are normally found on easily-defensible coastal headlands, across which a series of banks and ditches can be constructed to defend the landward side of the fort. The Dunpower promontary fort has three banks and ditches, which were cut across the narrowest part of the headland; the precipitous cliffs on three sides providing an excellent defence from seaborne attack. The inhospitable location of many of these sites suggests they were places of temporary refuge, only occupied in times of conflict.

AGRICULTURE

Farming was perhaps the single most important activity in early medieval Ireland. The greater part of the population would have been directly involved in it, and the whole tenor of everyday life both in the monasteries and in secular settlements would have revolved around the agricultural cycle. Cattle had a very special significance for the early Irish. Dairy products were an essential part of their diet, and, as cows yielded milk, every aspect of their care ensured that nothing should prevent them from doing so. Most bull calves, other than those needed for breeding or for traction, were probably slaughtered at birth, whilst calves were carefully separated from the cows so as to ensure that most of the milk was available for human consumption. Other domesticated animals (principally sheep and pigs) were also important, although significantly less so than cattle. Indeed, it is difficult to underestimate the importance of animal husbandry in early Irish agriculture. Yet the agricultural economy of early medieval Ireland was based on mixed farming, with cereal crops such as barley, oats and wheat being grown in sizeable quantities in the same period.

It is now a virtually standard practice for archaeological deposits from Irish sites to be carefully screened by specialists, whose painstaking task it is to identify the remains of any crops which may have been consumed on a site. Early Irish literature also provides us with many references to the types of cereals grown in this period, and the way in which they were planted, harvested and prepared for eating. Hand-operated mills (rotary querns) have been discovered with such frequency on settlement sites of the period that there can be little doubt that cereals were an everyday item of contemporary diet. Grain-drying kilns and water-powered grain mills were also common throughout the Irish countryside in the same period, which suggests not only that larger crops were being harvested but that they were also being more widely distributed. The construction of a watermill, as we shall see, represents a sizeable investment, and is one which would not have been undertaken unless the level of production involved made it worthwhile.

THE LITTLE ISLAND WATERMILLS

Water-powered milling has a special significance in the early medieval archaeology of the Cork harbour area, as one early medieval water-powered mill site investigated on Little Island has proved to be of both national and international importance. In 1979 clearance work associated with the excavation of large storage lagoons for Mitsui-Denman Ireland, on Little Island, revealed the remains of two early 7th-century watermills. One of these was a horizontal-wheeled mill, a type of mill quite common in Ireland during the early medieval period, and which survived in a number of north eastern counties up until quite recent times.

In horizontal-wheeled mills the water wheel, as the name suggests, is set in the horizontal plane and the shaft driving the millstones is set vertically. A small stream was often impounded by a rudimentary dam to form a millpond, from which water was led in an open channel to the millworks. Before the water was allowed to strike the waterwheel it was directed into a large chute hollowed-out from a tree-trunk. The internal area of the chute was deliberately shaped so as to increase the velocity of the water passing through it, while a crude nozzle bored through the front of it ensured that the water leaving it was more efficiently directed upon the paddles of the waterwheel. The

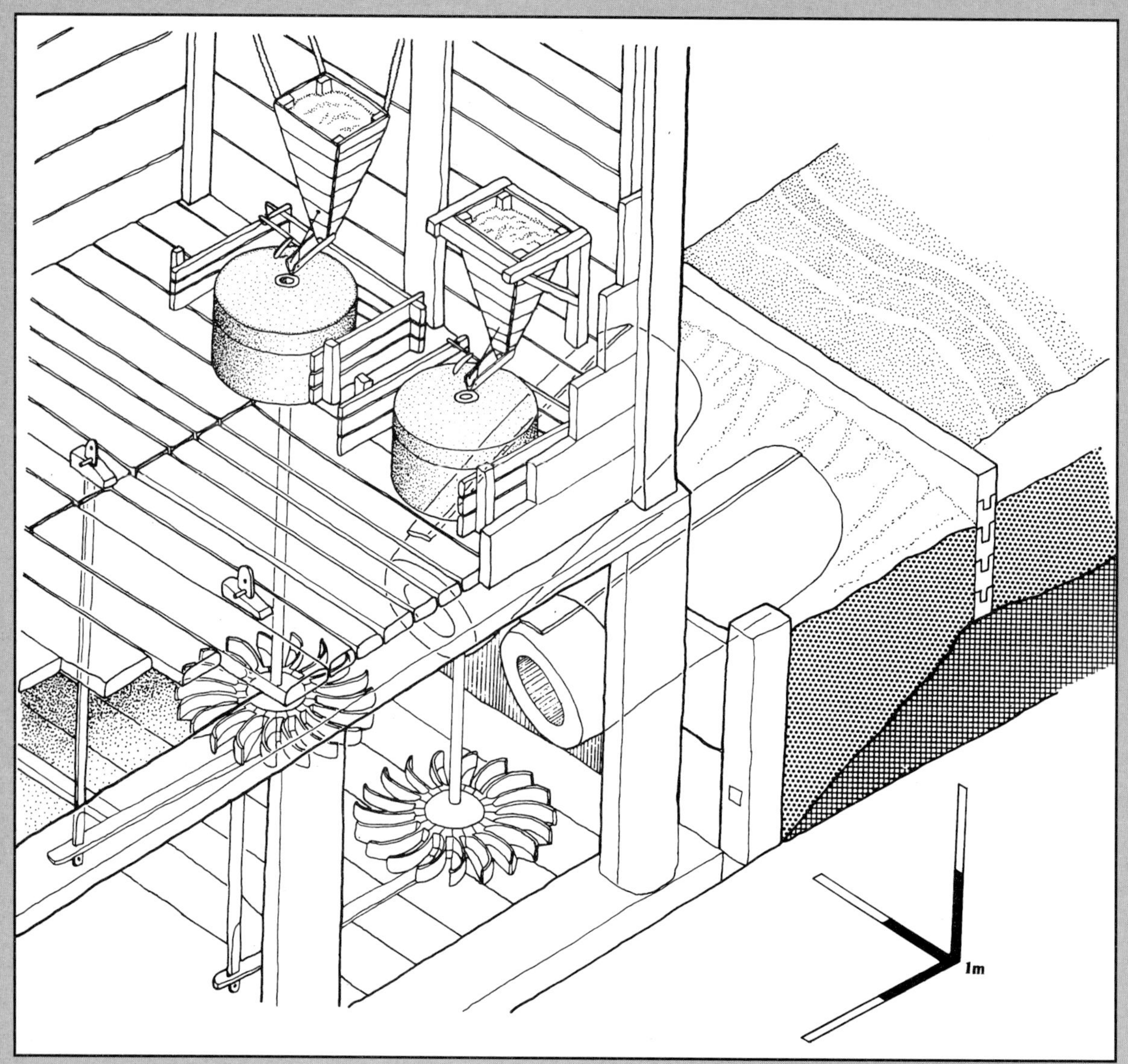

30. Reconstruction of 7th century, horizontal-wheeled watermill at Little Island, Co. Cork. This is the earliest example of its type yet to come to light in Europe.

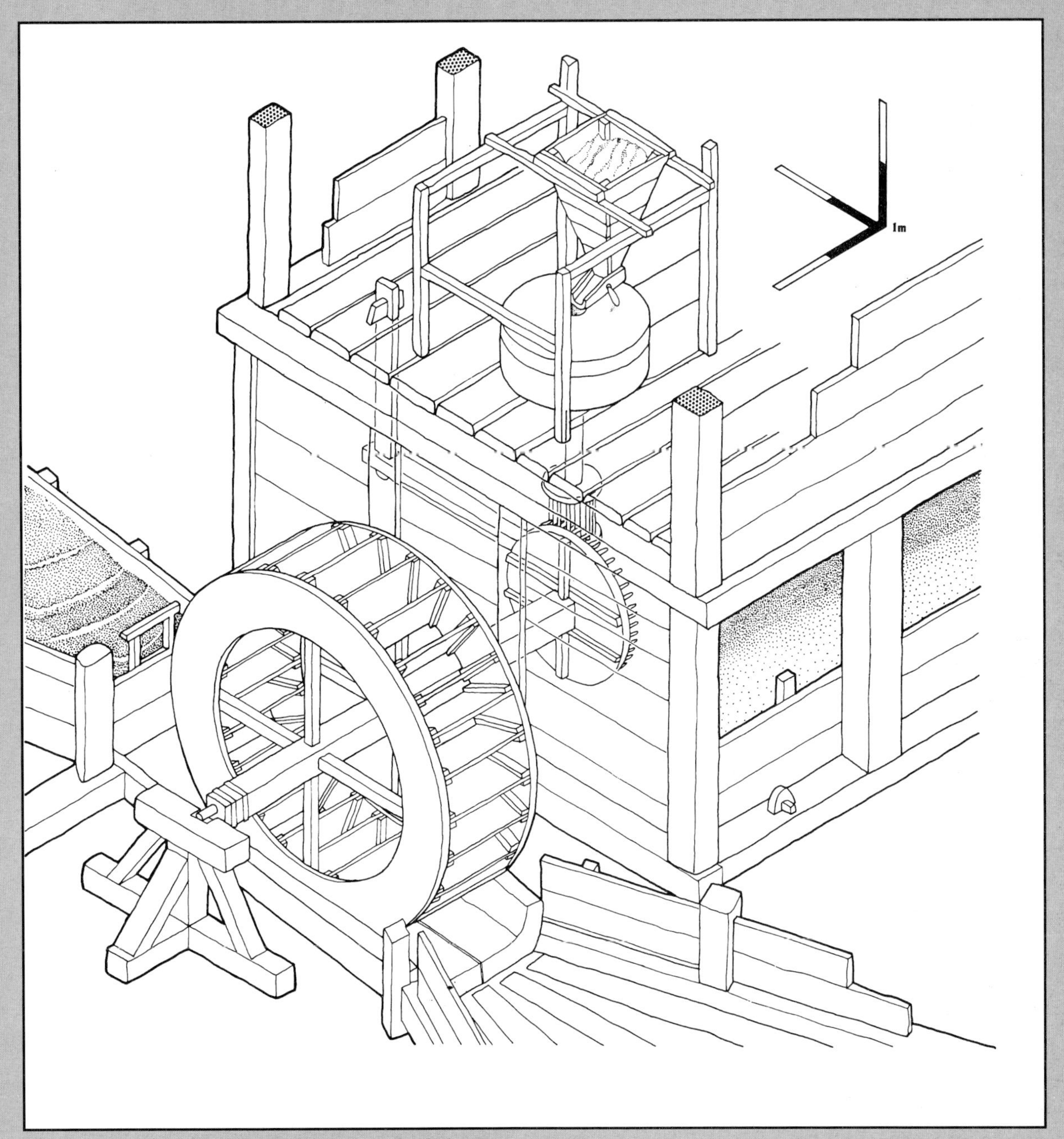

31. Reconstruction of 7th-century, vertical-wheeled water-mill at Little Island, Co. Cork. This is the earliest example of its type yet to come to light in Ireland.

waterwheel would have had anything from 19 to 24 spoon-shaped paddles, carefully shaped so as to ensure that they could more efficiently absorb the force of the water jet directed upon them.

The vast majority of the Irish horizontal-wheeled mills of this period operated with a single waterwheel, but there are at least six examples- of which Little Island is the earliest-which are likely to have operated with two. In each case the chutes would have serviced separate waterwheels, which would have powered individual pairs of millstones. On the analogy of similar mills found throughout Europe in more recent times, the rationale behind housing two waterwheels, as it were, under the one roof, appears to have been the desire to make the most of a good mill site. In Europe and Asia the siting of large numbers of mills in close proximity to each other, on the same water source, was quite common; with the water being used in succession by any number of mills. In certain areas a particularly good site was utilised by building a single mill and housing anything from two to six waterwheels (each serviced by a separate chute) in the same building.

No remains of the original waterwheels were discovered in the rescue excavation of 1979. That at least one of these mills was horizontal-wheeled was clear enough, but the second mill structure was somewhat more problematical. This mill had tapered wooden inlet and outlet channels which converged inwards and outwards, respectively, from a centrally placed trough. The floor of the inlet channel immediately in front of the trough had a wattle mat made of willow twigs, which was held in place by a series of wooden pegs. Its purpose appears to have been to limit the scouring action of the incoming water which is likely to have eroded the mud underneath the trough. The trough itself was a two-piece construction, a little over 3m long, 1.3m wide at rear end, and was "stitched" together on its underside with wooden clamps. It was all too evident that this trough could not have been used to direct water onto a horizontal waterwheel. The tell-tale, v-shaped configuration of the inlet and outlet channels of the mill, indeed, and the central position of the trough, suggested that a vertical waterwheel of the undershot type had been used.

In vertical wheeled water-mills - the type with which most people would be familiar - the axle is set horizontally. As the millstones were positioned in a different plane to that of the waterwheel's axle, the motion of the waterwheel could not be directly transmitted to them. Thus at least two gear wheels, one set on the waterwheel's axle and the other at right angles to it, were needed to transfer this motion to the upper millstone. In undershot waterwheels incoming water is directed onto the lowest part of the wheel's circumference. It is the impact rather than the weight of the water acting upon the paddles which sets the wheel in motion, and to this end the trough in undershot mills performs two essential tasks. As in horizontal-wheeled mills the full force of the water is needed to set the wheel in motion, but here the analogy ends. For in vertical undershot mills the waterwheel is positioned directly over the trough, which not only directs water onto the paddles, but prevents it from escaping around their sides. The purpose of the outward tapering channel is to lead the water away from the wheel, for if water is allowed to linger in the trough it will impede the rotation of the waterwheel.

The Little Island watermills are the earliest known examples of either type to come to light in Ireland. Indeed, up until quite recently it was thought that vertical-wheeled mills were not used in Ireland until the 12th century A.D. Both mills have been dated by dendrochronology (tree-ring dating) to the year A.D. 630, and there can now be little doubt that both horizontal and vertical-wheeled mills were in use in Ireland by at least the early decades of the 7th century A.D. This is the earliest known close association of each type of watermill from anywhere in early medieval Europe, whilst the double chute horizontal-wheeled mill is the earliest known example of its type in either Europe or Asia. But the most truly remarkable aspect of the Little Island discovery was the area which the builders had chosen for siting the mills, and the likely means by which the mills were supplied with water.

EUROPE'S EARLIEST TIDE MILLS?

In the 7th century A.D. Little Island would have been in certain respects very different from what it is today. To begin with, it would have been a true island with extensive areas of tidal marsh around its shoreline, and the estuarine waters of Lough Mahon would have intruded much further inland than they do today. The area in which the mills had been discovered was reclaimed in the late 18th century, and by the early decades of the 19th century most of the marshy areas on the island had been drained. The mill site is approximately 250m from the present shoreline, but as the estuarine deposits which eventually destroyed the site clearly indicate, this would not have been the case in the early 7th century. The foundations of these mills were covered by up to 1.5m of estuarine gravel and mud, which suggests not only that the site was eventually destroyed by tidal flooding, but that in the period when these mills were built the tidal waters of Lough Mahon extended inland as far as the mill site itself. Furthermore, the foundations of the mills had been built on riverine mud, which can only suggest that the mills had been built on what was then a tidal marsh.

On the face of it this would appear to be a disastrous choice of mill site. In other circumstances the island location would be understandable, if fast flowing streams running down from an upland area were available. Yet Little Island is one of the most low-lying areas in Cork Harbour. We cannot as yet entirely rule out the possibilty that this small, low-lying island had streams large enough in the early 7th century to power two large watermills. If a fresh water supply was ever intended for these mills, why build them in an exposed area which was subject to severe tidal flooding? The daily ebb and flow of the tides would have severely interrupted the flow of any supply of fresh water led into the area in which these mills were built. If it was the intention of the builders to tap fresh water streams, then clearly they would have sited these mills well away from areas upon which the tides encroached.

The choice of the Little Island site was clearly not accidental: the builders were fully aware of the risks involved in building a complex of this size in such a location. Whereas the foundation beams of more conventional early Irish watermills were simply laid on the ground, those at Little Island were firmly pinned to the mud with substantial oaken piles over 2m long. The scale of the carpentry involved at Little Island has, in fact, more in common with medieval quaysides of ports such as Dublin or, indeed, London. It is perhaps no coincidence that the closest parallels for the type of piling using at Little Island are to be found in structures which were subjected to the scouring action of the tides. So how could the builders of these mills' site possibly gain from choosing this location? The answer to this question appears to lie in the mills' proximity to the estuarine waters of Lough Mahon. In a twelve-hour cycle the tide ebbs and flows, and in the early 7th century A.D. the area around the mills would have been inundated by the waters of Lough Mahon. As in the case of other mills constructed in similar locations, the likelihood is that these were *tide mills:* mills which exploited the daily ebb and flow of the tides to fill their millponds. The millponds would have been filled on the flow tide, and the mills would have been operated when the tide went out, whereupon their ponds would have been replemished when the tide rose again.

Similar mills - with both horizontal and vertical waterwheels - are known to have been at work on the Atlantic coasts of France, Britain, Spain, Portugal and Holland from at least the medieval period onwards. Some of these were in existence up until quite recent times and a small number are still operated. Their ultimate origin is unknown, and the earliest historical record of their use occurs in a 10th century work by the Arab geographer al- Muqaddasi:

The tide is a marvel and blessing for the people of Basra. [on the Persian Gulf] The water visits them twice every day, and it enters the rivers... And when the tide ebbs it is also useful for the working of mills because they are situated at the mouth of the river and its tributaries.

Accounts of English tide mills from the late 13th century onwards underline the hazards of siting tide mills on or near estuaries, where storms and high tides often destroyed or severely damaged mills. A late 13th century tide mill on the Isle of Thanet in Kent, for example, which appears to have had a similar location to that of the Little Island mills, was apparently destroyed by tidal flooding in the late 13th century. Henry of Eastry, the Prior of Christ Church, Canterbury (1285-1331), had it replaced for the then enormous sum of £114 13s, but the mill was again damaged by floods in 1316. It was then moved to another site, but was again destroyed by high tides in 1326; and eventually continual damage to the mill forced its removal to a safer, inland site. At Little Island tidal flooding appears to have been a continual hazard, and there is even evidence to suggest that some repairs (possibly resulting from this) were made during its period of use. Severe flooding, indeed, may well have led to the eventual abandonment of the site.

Within the last two decades a large number of early medieval, horizontal-wheeled mill sites have come to light in Ireland. But none of these can in any way match the scale of operations at Little Island. The site itself is as much a testament to the ambition of its builders as it is to the tradition from which it sprung. For not only does the Little Island discovery push back the origins of tide mills in Europe by some three centuries, it also provides us with clear-cut evidence of the advanced nature of millwrighting in Ireland during the early 7th century. In the present state of our knowledge we have no way of knowing how common similarly located mills were in the same period. On the balance of probability it was neither the first nor the last site of its type to be constructed in early medieval Europe.

How then, and by whom, did such a complex come to be built in the estuary of the River Lee? Clearly we are dealing here with a movement of ideas as well as commodities from continental Europe, and the Little Island mills leave us in little doubt that such exchanges, in our area of interest, were already well underway by the early 7th century. There is other archaeological evidence for long distance trade with Europe during this period, but the exchanges largely involved commodities such as wine which could not be produced in Ireland. The construction of water-powered mills, however, needs only locally procured building materials and know-how. Yet the existence of the necessary skills is in itself not enough to ensure that such mills will be built. For there must also be a perceived need for them, a climate of opinion that accepts these skills should be put to good use, if not for the benefit of all, then at least by those who can afford to use them. We will probably never know who owned these mills, but there can be no doubt that it was within their power to marshal the resources needed for this task, and that it was in their immediate interest to do so. Whoever they were, it is highly unlikely that they built these mills to process small quantities of cereals, and so the very existence of these mills strongly suggests that large crops were being harvested in at least some areas of the harbour in the 7th century.

THE EARLY MEDIEVAL IRISH CHURCH

In the south of Ireland there are a number of local legends which suggest that Christian missionaries were at work before St Patrick. The *Corcu Loigde,* for example, a tribe whose ancestral territory covered most of what is latterly the modern dioceses of Ross, are said to have been the first people in Ireland to receive the faith. Around the turn of the 5th century A.D., St Ciaran of Cape Clear is said to have returned from the continent, after taking holy orders there, and to have begun to convert his native west Cork to Christianity. St Patrick's successors were clearly better publicists than those of Ciaran, and in popular tradition the conversion of Ireland is commonly portrayed as a single-handed effort by Patrick. There is other evidence which, while it does not directly establish the existence of "pre-Patrician" saints in Ireland, does point to the existence of Christian communities here before the mission of St. Patrick.

In A.D. 431 bishop Palladius was dispatched by Pope Celestine "to the Irish believing in Christ". The event is recorded in a European chronicle, but no memory or acknowledgement of it is recorded in the Irish sources: Palladius may have come and gone but if he did so he was not remembered. But even before Palladius' mission the Irish were already borrowing Latin words, and incorporating them into their own language. Most of these "loan words", it is true, suggest that the borrowings arose out of trading contacts, but others are clearly of a religious nature. That such words were in use by the early 5th century A.D. can only suggest that they formed part of the vocabulary of Irish Christians. We have no idea how these small groups were organised, how they worshipped or, indeed, the extent to which their survival was based on tolerance. Indeed, even the means by which Christianity was introduced into Ireland are not fully understood, and it is generally assumed that proximity to Britain provided the impetus for this development.

The earliest Irish Church is likely to have been organised in a diocesan system, in which a bishop held sway over a number of recognised Christian communities. The dioceses, being first and foremost a Roman administrative unit, appears not to have been to Irish tastes. Thus in the 6th century we find that a monastic system based on *paruchiae* ("federations" of subject monasteries, each controlled by a motherhouse) are beginning to replace dioceses as the principal form of Irish ecclesiastical organisation. In this system, which had all but replaced the diocesan model by the 7th century, it was the abbot of a monastery rather than the bishop who held sway over the faithful. From the viewpoint of the European Church this form of organisation was, to the say the least, unorthodox. But in Irish eyes this was a necessary and ultimately an acceptable compromise, through which the Church could graft itself upon early Irish society.

THE ARCHAEOLOGY OF THE EARLY CHURCH IN THE CORK HARBOUR AREA

Time and progress have poorly served the archaeology of the early Church within our area of interest: there are no surviving early medieval church sites, and few extant remains of buildings known to have been associated with them. With the exception of Cloyne, founded by Colman mac Lenine in the 6th century, all of the early monastic foundations within the environs of the harbour are 7th century. In the first decade of the 7th century a monastery was established on the south bank of the River Lee at Cork. No saint is more closely associated with the monastery of *Corcagh mór* than Finbarr, and the foundation of its first monastery is traditionally attributed to him. The traditional account of his life and works has been gleaned from official biographies, compiled many hundreds of years after the period in which he is presumed to have lived. Thus we cannot expect that their contents in any way accurately represent the life and times of their chosen subject. But there are other reasons for being wary of their contents. For in the 12th century, when many of these saints' lives were compiled, the reason for doing so was generally for propaganda purposes rather than religious instruction. While cynics may profess to see no difference between these, it is clear that by this period many monasteries were prepared to produce biographies of their founding saints to claim ownership and control of other foundations. The life of St Finbarr follows a very similar pattern, in that it provides a detailed account of the property and affiliated churches which the 12th century monastery at Cork claimed as its own. Herein lies its real value: for as an accurate account of the life of and work of St. Finbarr it has none. At best it is part of a legend rescued from obscurity and superimposed upon a recognisable landscape, the landscape of Cork.

So what can we actually claim to know about St Finbarr of Cork? Our earliest evidence for Finbarr's association with Cork actually dates from the 8th century: but what was the nature of that association? As has been recently and convincingly argued, St Finbarr's connection with the foundation of the monastery of Cork is the stuff of legend. Finbarr, also known as Finnian, was noted for his holiness and erudition, and was adopted by devotees all over Ireland and Britain. Variations of his name were used in the areas in which his cult (from the latin *cultus* "worship") was adopted, and in Cork he was first known under the name of *Bairrfhionn* from which the form *Bairre* was later derived. And, as in other areas in which his cult was adopted, the life and works of the saint were provided with a local setting.

St. Finbarr's association with the monastery at Cork, then, appears to have had nothing to do with a saint called Bairrfhionn - or any of the many variants of this name used by devotees elsewhere - having been anywhere near the site. The monks of Cork simply adopted a popular, widely respected saint as their patron who in later centuries came to be credited with the foundation of the site.

THE MONASTERY OF ST.FINBARR

The exact location of the monastery of Cork is unknown, although the existence of a round tower near the site of the present St Finbarr's cathedral could suggest that the early monastery was situated here. Round towers can be dated to the period between the 9th and 12th centuries A.D., and it may well be that the round tower at Cork was built within an earlier ecclesiastical enclosure. Tall, circular structures, which taper upwards from the base in the direction of the ingeniously corbelled conical "cap" which surmounts the top, Irish round towers were monastic status symbols. The round tower at Cork would have been visible for miles around and, like similar structures at other Irish monastic sites, it was probably intended to be an outward symbol of the monastery's wealth and importance. The term *cloigtech* ("belfry"), which is often used in the early medieval sources, provides some indication of their original function, though hand-held rather than hanging bells (like those found in more recent church steeples) are likely to have been used. They also appear to have functioned both as refuges and storehouses for monastic valuables, and the positioning of their doorways well above ground level appears to be consistent with this idea.

The round tower at Cork is depicted on the earliest known maps of the city, and was briefly described by the French traveller Boullaye le Gouz, who had visited Cork in 1644. A monstrance made in 1669, currently in the Dominican Friary on Pope's Quay, has an engraving of St Finbarr ("S.Barrey") on its foot which depicts a capless round tower. The tower is presumably a representation of that then existing at Cork, which is shown to have a round-headed doorway with seven windows set vertically in line above it. Irish round towers could also have up to eight storeys, access to which was by means of internal wooden ladders; and if the Pope's Quay monstrance is anything to go on the Cork tower may have had seven storeys. It is commonly held that this tower was used as a sniping position by English troops during the siege of Cork in 1690, and that the tower was damaged by retaliatory fire from Elizabeth Fort. The evidence from contemporary accounts of the siege, however, clearly indicates that the English snipers took up position on the steeple of the then cathedral of St Finbarr. The round tower is thought to have collapsed of its own volition early in the 18th century, and no traces of it have survived.

We are almost completely in the dark as to the layout and size of the early monastery at Cork. From at least the 12th century onwards there appears to have always been a church or cathedral to St. Finbarr on or near the site of the present cathedral. There are, in fact, some surviving 12th-century worked building stones from the site which are likely to have been part of an early medieval church. The round tower, like that surviving at Cloyne (see below), gives us some idea of the monastery's wealth and importance. Yet there are few indications that Cork was considered in its heyday to be a "monastic city" in the same way as other important monastic centres such as Armagh or Clonmcanoise. Nonetheless, it was considered by contemporaries to be, along with Armagh, Clonmacnoise, Kildare and Bangor, one of Ireland's most important monastic schools; and was among a small number of Irish monasteries which became bishoprics. Doubtless it may not have matched the other centres of learning in terms of its size, though the monastery is likely to have provided the spur for the growth of secular settlements within its immediate environs. Like other important early medieval monastic sites it was established in a location with direct access to a navigable river. The River Lee at this point provided ready access to the sea and to the interior, and the monastery would no doubt have hoped to use its accessibility to its best advantage.

In A.D. 807 the *familia* or monastic community at Cork were involved in a battle with the *familia* of Clonfert, Co. Galway. The idea of monks going to war, to modern eyes, is not without its humorous side, but in such cases the term *familia* ("household") had more than spiritual overtones. For more often than not tribal loyalties to local kings or chieftains would take precedence over spritual ones. On this occasion it seems that the *familia* of Cork were not prepared to turn the other cheek, but on the day appear to have come off the worse in the encounter. Just over a century later, in 908, no less a personage than the Abbot of Cork was reported killed in the Battle of Bealach Mughna fighting for King Cormac of Cashel. The idea of an important monastic official forming part of a war hosting does not seem to have unduly troubled contemporaries. In fact they would have expected it. The Abbot of Cork was clearly doing his duty to his king by his presence on the battlefield, where he was all too obviously not a spectator. The battle between Clonfert and Cork is particularly interesting, because it seems that both the monastic administrators and the *manaig* took an active part in the affray. The manaig, or lay monks, were an essential part of the monastic community who farmed the land owned by the monastery. They lived with their wives and families on the monastic estate and were allowed certain priviledges in return; and in Cork, as in early monastic communities elsewhere, they may well have formed the nucleus of a secular settlement associated with the monastery. The monastery would also have attracted skilled craftsmen such as metalworkers, carpenters and shipwrights, who would also have swelled its number of dependents.

CLOYNE

The round tower at Cloyne is the only early medieval monastic building to have survived within the harbour area. The tower is of locally quarried sandstone, 5.17m wide at the base, and in its present state over 30m high. There are seven storeys, with a small window to each of these. During the last century a bronze cross, dating to the early 12th century, was discovered in the chapter house of Cloyne cathedral. The art style of the figures on each of its arms shows some Scandinavian influences, whilst the figures themselves are very similar to those on the Lismore crozier. Indeed, the similarity between the figures on the Cloyne cross and those on the Lismore crozier (c.A.D. 1090-1113) is so close that it has been suggested that they may well be the work of the same craftsman. With regard to the cross's original function, the holes punched at the end of each of its arms would suggest that it originally formed part of a book shrine.

The only other early church sites within the harbour area (which are thought to have been established in the early 7th century) are the monastery of Inis Pic (Spike Island) and the church of Rosbeg near Ringaskiddy. These are associated with St Mochua (Carthage) of Lismore, who is said to have travelled through

32. Round Tower at Cloyne, Co. Cork.

33. *Cloyne cross, early 12th-century.*

34. *Detail of Cloyne cross. Its style of decoration shows some Scandinavian influences.*

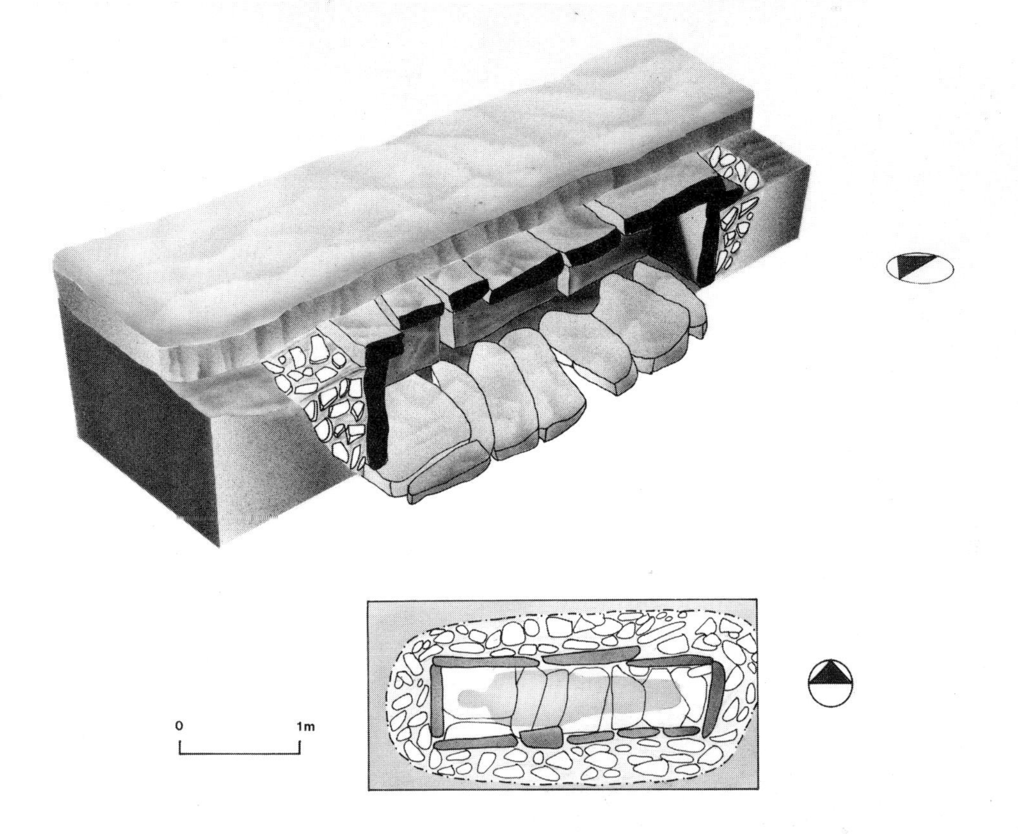

35. Long cist at Hoddersfield, Co. Cork.

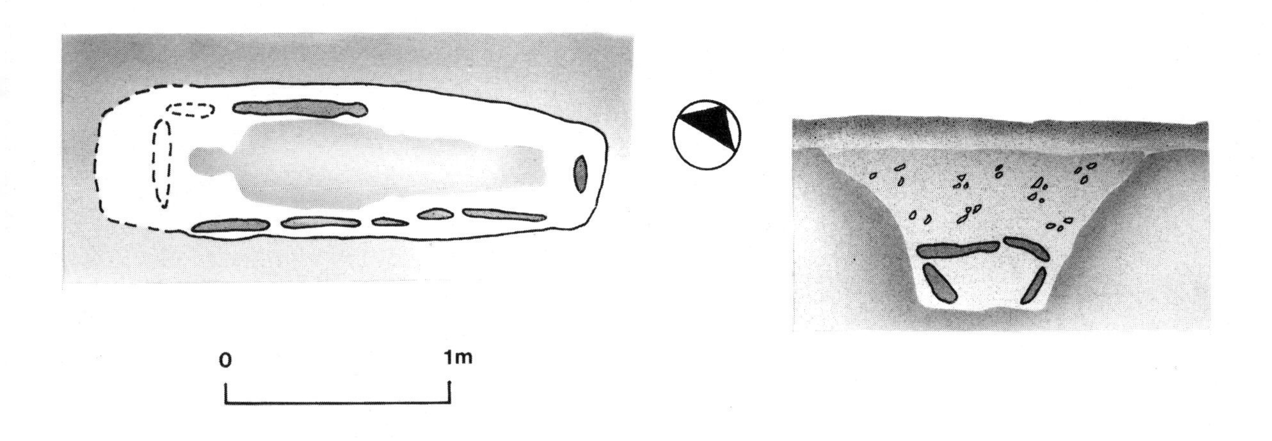

36. Long cist at Coppingerstown, Co. Cork.

37. Spindle whorls from Ravenswood, near Carrigaline, Co. Cork. The larger example is of fine-grained sandstone and is 5.5cm in diameter. The other example is made from limestone, diameter 3.4cm.

the latter day barony of Kerrycurrihy on the western side of the harbour, when Cathal Mac Aedha (d.620) was King of Munster. The stone foundations of the Rosbeg church site appear to have survived within the orchard of Ballybricken House as late as 1700. But today neither site survives, nor are they shown on the earliest maps of the harbour.

BURIALS

To-date no early Christian cemeteries or cross-slab grave markers, typical of early Christian burials, have come to light in the Cork harbour area. There are, however, two long cist grave burials which have been investigated at Hoddersfield, near Crosshaven, and Coppingerstown near the Ballynacorra-Castlemartyr road. The sides of the Hoddersfield cist were defined by massive sandstone slabs, and the area enclosed by them had been floored with similar flags. The grave contained the remains of a tall, well-built adult male aprroximately 23-40 years of age, and was covered by six sandstone slabs. In comparison, the Coppingerstown example was quite poorly constructed. Its male occupant was of similar physique to that of the Hoddersfield grave, but was somewhat older, perhaps middle-aged. Where graves of this type are concerned their orientation (which is generally W-E) and the fact that neither weapons nor jewelry are buried with the deceased, is normally taken as an indication that the burial is Christian. The head, it is generally assumed, as in the case of the Hoddersfield cist, is laid at the west; so that at the ressurection the body would be facing eastwards in the direction of the Holy Land. On present evidence, when burials of this type are found in cemeteries, they generally date to the

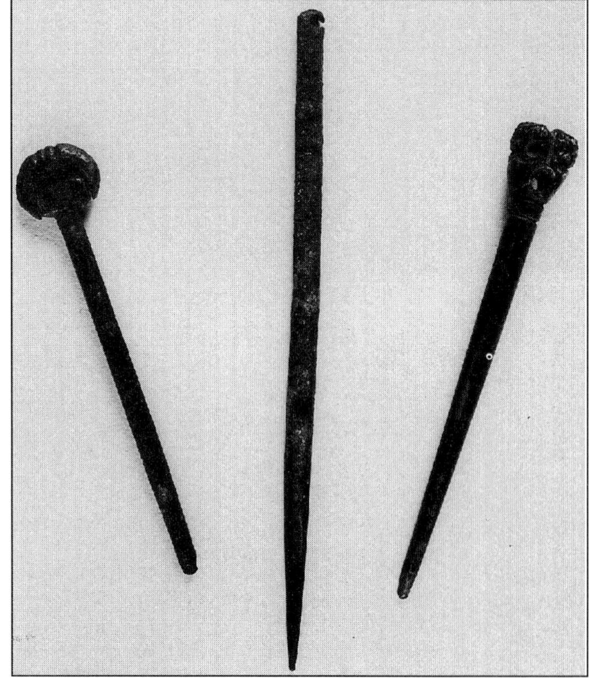

38. Early-medieval bronze pins from Carrigaline, Co. Cork: left, ring-headed pin (8.5cm long); centre, plain pin (11.3cm long), right, pin with ornamented knob (8.3cm long).

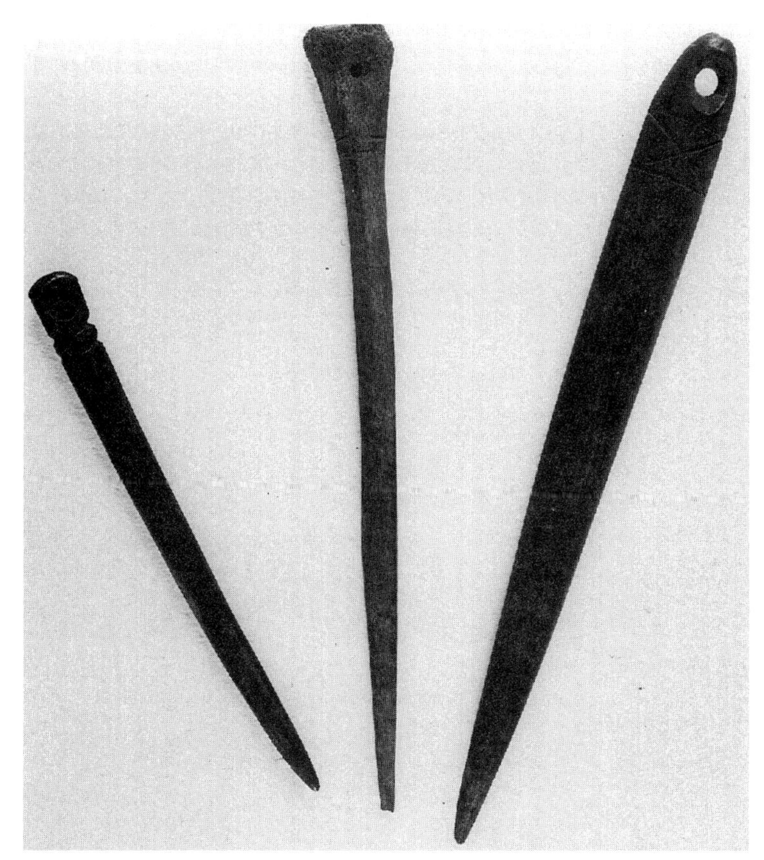

39. Early medieval ornamented bone pins from Carrigaline, Co. Cork. Left, 5cm long; centre, 9.5cm long; right, 10.1cm long.

40. Carved stone head from Trabolgan, Co. Cork.

7th century or later, but there is no certainty about this where isolated burials of the Hoddersfield or Coppingerstown type are concerned. The likelihood is, however, that burials of this type are of early medieval date, but we cannot safely assume that all were inspired by Christian rites.

CRAFTS

Only a small number of artefacts dating from this period have been discovered in the harbour area, and most of these are "stray finds". These include a series of bone and bronze pins and stone spindle whorls from the Carrigaline area, all of which would have been everyday items in the early medieval period. A spindle whorl is simply a stone with a hole in the centre, which enabled it to be attached to the top of the spindle used in the hand-spinning of either wool or linen. The women in the early medieval household would have toiled long hours at this task, and doubtless would have also been reponsible for weaving the woollen or linen yarn into cloth. We know very little about the main styles of dress in this period, though it seems that the nobility would have worn either ankle or knee-length linen tunics. For all classes of society in early Ireland one of the most important garments was the *brat* or mantle, which was worn around the shoulders or on the chest. Both bone and bronze pins, like those recovered from the harbour area, were used as dress-fasteners to hold them in place. One of the Cork harbour examples is a simple ring pin which, in its day, would have been a down-market version of the Tara brooch. Needless to say the bone pins would have figured even lower in this scheme of things, and these are likely to have been worn by the less well-off. None of these pins can be closely dated, and all that can be said about them with any certainty is that they date to the period from the 9th to the 12th centuries; in other words to the later part of the early medieval period.

One of the most interesting discoveries in recent years is the carved stone head, accidentally discovered in the ditch of a rath at Trabolgan. It is carved out of a sandstone pebble and would fit quite comfortably into the palm of one's hand. The Trabolgan head is unlike other miniature stone sculptures of the late Iron Age and current opinion (such as it is) favours an early medieval date for it. Ornament or charm? Pagan or Christian? In the present state of our knowledge it is impossible to tell.

FOREIGN TRADE

We have already seen how early medieval pottery of French origin came to light during the Raheens excavations. This is not the first evidence for trade between the greater Cork area and the continent during the early medieval period, and will undoubtedly not be the last. Earthen raths at Garryduff and Garranes in County Cork have produced exotic pottery of Mediterranean origin, and the likelihood is that this trade was conducted through Cork harbour. It may well have been associated with imports of wine or olive oil, but whatever commodities were involved the evidence for this long-distance trade is unmistakable. Fragments of large storage vessels called *amphorae,* for example, which came from North Africa, have been discovered during rath excavations in Cork county. The amphorae can be dated to the 4th and 5th centuries A.D. and are now thought to represent an early period of long-distance trade between Ireland, Britain and the Mediterranean. This was followed in the 6th and 7th centuries by trade in a type of domestic pottery commonly referred to as "E-ware", which has also come to light in the greater Cork area. A location somewhere in north central France is presently believed to be the origin of E-ware, but it has not yet been possible to pinpoint this exactly. Its appearance in Ireland is generally taken as evidence for a trade in wine with France, the wine itself being transported in barrels and the pottery vessels serving as a second cargo. We also know from documentary sources that a trade in wine between Ireland and France was conducted in this period, whilst Irish clerics are known to have travelled to the continent and vice versa. And, as we shall see later, this type of trade between Cork and the continent was considerably expanded in the medieval period.

THE VIKINGS

Towards the end of the 8th century the wealth of Ireland's monasteries attracted the unwelcome attention of Viking raiders, and by the early decades of the 9th century raids were becoming a frequent occurrence. There could have been little organised resistance to these attacks, and monasteries in coastal locations proved easy prey for sea borne raiders. The important monastic foundation at Armagh, for example, was raided no less than three times in the year A.D.832. No doubt the spoils involved and the vulnerability of their main targets encouraged the raiders to make return visits. That they did find reason to do so suggests that certain monasteries had been able to repair most of the damage caused by earlier raids.

The monastery of St Finbarr at Cork was attacked and plundered in A.D. 820. There is no record of any further attacks until 838, and in all only three Viking attacks are recorded in a three-hundred-and-fifty year period. Cloyne, on the other hand, owing to its proximity to the harbour, was frequently raided. Its monastery was attacked six times between 821 and 885, and in the last recorded raid the abbot, prior and other monks were actually killed. Indeed, the damage appears to have been lasting, because from 885 onwards there are no documentary references to the monastery at Cloyne for almost two centuries.

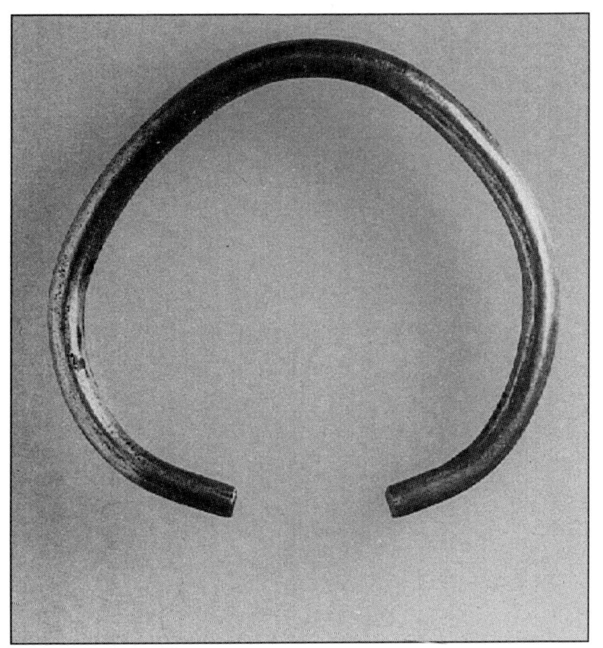

41. Viking Silver armring from Kilbarry Co. Cork

In 846 the king of Munster Olchobar mac Cinaeda attacked the dun corcaighe, the Viking fortress at Cork, which is the first indication we have that a fortified Viking settlement existed at Cork. The monastic settlement at Cork with its easy access to the harbour, its trading network and the lack of any serious opposition, may have encouraged a raiding party to winter at Cork. What may well have begun as a temporary base later developed into a fortified Viking settlement, the *dun corcaighe.* Yet there appears to have been a limit to which the Irish were prepared to tolerate their presence. The *caisteol* ("castle") of the Vikings at Cork is said to have been destroyed by them in 865, when the leader of the Cork Vikings, Gnimbeolu, was killed. The Viking presence at Cork after this date all but disappears from the documentary sources. Then, in A.D. 914, the monastery at Cork was plundered by a Viking fleet raiding in Munster, with some of the raiders opting to settle at Cork. It is possible that in this period the Cork Vikings expelled the *Ciarraighe Cuirche* (the people who gave their name to the modern barony of Kerrycurrihy), from their lands to the south-west of the harbour. At any rate there are no references to the Ciarriaghe Cuirche after the 10th century.

THE VIKING SETTLEMENT AT CORK

The Scandinavians who settled at Cork appear to have done so with the consent of the monastery, for once they became established at Cork they clearly chose not to interfere with it. We find the same state of affairs in the Scandinavian settlements around Dublin where the Vikings appear to have co-existed with the local church. This would have been a satisfactory arrangement for both parties, each of which would have had much to gain from being linked into the Scandinavian trade network. In any case the "foreigners", as they are called in the contemporary Irish accounts, eventually blended in with their surroundings. Their legacy to the society into which they were absorbed included (amongst other things) some of the earliest Irish towns and the first Irish coinage. In spite of this their descendents in Ireland were unable to maintain either their lands or their separate indentity after the arrival of the Anglo Normans (see below).

To-date the Viking settlement at Cork has proved to be the most accomplished archaeological vanishing act. In Dublin, Wexford and Waterford the remains of Scandinavian settlements have been excavated, and only in Cork have they proven to be elusive. Attempts have been made to pinpoint the area of the Viking settlement at Cork using written sources, but at best these can only provide the haziest of outlines. From these it appears that Viking Cork was situated on the south island, and spread south of the river into the present-day Sullivan's Quay and Barrack Street area of the city. Little more than this can be said with any degree of certainty, for archaeological excavation within the precincts of the medieval city is a matter of opportunity rather than choice. The only sites which can be excavated in the city are those which are scheduled for development, and few of these have occurred in the areas we would expect to find the Viking settlement. As luck would have it none of the sites excavated to-date have produced Viking deposits. However, many of these excavations, particularly on the south island, have concentrated on the city walls. By the time these were built the extent of the medieval city extended well beyond that established by the Vikings, and so we should not be too surprised when the archaeological deposits near the city walls prove to be later than the period of the Viking settlement. Furthermore, only a very small area of the medieval city has been excavated. If we take the the area within the medieval city walls as one large archaeological site, then the area of it that has been excavated, in relative terms, is quite small, and can by no means be considered representative of the entire city during this period. Bearing this in mind, the fact that the remains of the Viking settlement at Cork have not yet come to light during excavations in the city is hardly surprising.

Up until quite recently the Viking towns of Ireland were seen as way-stations for Viking trade, and bases for attack on the surrounding countryside. Like all urban areas, these towns would have relied quite heavily on their environs for everyday commodities such as food and building materials. The lands wrested from the Ciarraighe Cuirche are likely to have provided agricultural produce and other commodities for the Viking settlement at Cork, though we find few traces of Viking activity have come to light in the general harbour area. Few Viking rural settlements in Britain and Ireland have been excavated, and for the most part the existence of Norse placenames has been used to identify areas of Viking settlement. Dunkettle, for example, on the east side of the harbour may well be derived from *Dun Ketil,* Ketil being a Norse personal name. Such placenames, however, in the greater Cork area are very rare, and previous attempts to plot the extent of Viking settlement have also been hampered by the scarcity of Viking-Age artefacts. To-date only two Viking coins, a silver armring and a gaming piece have been found within the city and its immediate environs. One of the coins is a silver penny of Anluf Guthfrithsson (939-941) minted at York, the other a silver penny of Eric Bloodaxe (947-9, 952-9) minted at Ruding. The silver armring was one of six found in a hoard of Viking-Age silver, accidentally discovered in 1844 during the digging of a drain near Kilbarry just to the north of the city. The Kilbarry armring was the only one of the original six to have survived, and is now in the Ashmolean Museum at Oxford. The gaming piece was found in the city excavations conducted during the 1970s, and is similar to the 10th and 11th century examples excavated in Dublin.

By the 12th century the inhabitants of the settlement at Cork would have been a mixture of Irish and Hiberno-Vikings (i.e. Vikings who had intermarried with the native Irish), by which time settlement would have been firmly established along the south bank of the River Lee and the south island. This was attacked on no less than five occasions between 960 and 1089 by the native Irish, and contemporary accounts tell us of the destruction of both the "houses and churches". Cork's trade and the wealth generated by it did not escape the notice of the local power brokers. We know, for example, that the MacCarthy kings of Desmond insisted on receiving a share of the town's maritime trade. They imposed tolls on goods traded at Cork, and right up until its capture by the Anglo-Normans, the trade of Cork appears to have been firmly under their control.

The archaeology of Cork harbour during the early medieval period, as has been seen above, while disappointing in some respects, is truly remarkable in others. It is in this period that we can begin to speak of a "port" of Cork, which was probably engaged in active trade with the Mediterranean region before the establishment of a Viking trading settlement. Maritime trade is also likely to have been further developed through the Viking connection, when the establishment of a Viking settlement on the islands would have effectively linked Cork into the extensive Scandinavian trading network. It was the wealth generated by towns such as Cork which made them the most important spoils of the Anglo-Norman settlement. Their potential was not lost on the Anglo-Normans when Cork, as we shall see in the next chapter, along with Ireland's other Viking ports, was singled out for special treatment.

THREE

Cork: A Medieval City and its Environs

The Anglo-Norman settlement of Ireland was a conquest of opportunity. It all began with an armed intervention to assist the King of Leinster, Diarmait MacMurrough, when the newcomers found that they could quickly put paid to any resistance the native Irish were prepared to offer. The Anglo-Normans wasted no time in following up their advantage, and what began as an armed intervention in the years 1169-70, developed into a full-blown conquest. Henry II moved quickly to ensure some of the spoils for the crown by reserving the Hiberno-Viking ports of Dublin, Waterford, Cork and Limerick for himself. Royal authority over Ireland was vested by him in his son John, and the reins were firmly pulled in on his more ambitious subjects in Ireland.

In 1173 the men of Cork received a taste of things to come when they were defeated at Youghal by an Anglo-Norman fleet. Their leader, Gilbert Mac Turgar, who seems to have been of Viking descent, was killed in the affray, and within four years the city of Cork itself was in Anglo-Norman hands. The town to which they laid seige in 1177 appears to have been fortified, and it appears to have been badly damaged during its capture. Henry II granted the kingdom of Cork to Milo de Cogan and Robert Fitzstephen who proceeded to seize the property of the Hiberno-Vikings or Ostmen and to banish them from the city. This marks the end of the Scandinavian legacy in Cork: their lands in Kerrycurrihy were also confiscated, and they effectively disappear from the written sources soon afterwards.

In other areas of Ireland the Normans immediately began to build fortifications to consolidate their newly acquired lands, but in the greater Cork area there is little evidence for early Anglo-Norman military earthworks or castles. Nonetheless, the lands around the harbour area were parcelled out to new colonists, and presumably some steps were taken to provide adequate defence for these. The threat of an Irish uprising was a very real one, and, if the first Anglo-Norman colonists may have been lax in building strongholds in the outlying rural districts, they appear to have wasted no time in improving the city's defences. By at least 1182 the south island was defended by either timber or stone walls. We do not know if these were simply additions to the early Hiberno-Viking defences, but whatever they were, they proved to be a timely precaution. For in 1182 the Anglo-Norman kingdom of Cork was in revolt, Milo de Cogan was killed and the Anglo-Norman garrison at Cork was under siege. This was a serious reversal of Anglo-Norman fortunes, but the siege was quickly lifted. By 1183 the colonists had acquired the fertile lowlands of the territories of Ui Meic Caille (Imokilly) to the west and Ui Liathain (Olethan) to the north of the city. Order was temporarily restored to the colony, but, with the growth of native Irish influence throughout the later medieval period, the city became a colonial outpost. In later centuries, indeed, it had to be almost entirely supplied by sea.

The Anglo-Normans extended the Hiberno-Norse town, enclosed it with impressive stone walls and created a truly medieval city complete with a main street, market and quaysides. Thus far it is the remains of this city, and not that of the Hiberno-Viking period, which have come to light in archaeological excavations. These excavations, as we shall now see, have provided amazing insights into the everyday lives of the inhabitants of Anglo-Norman Cork. But let us first examine the relationship between the modern city and that preserved beneath its streets.

THE CITY BENEATH THE PAVEMENT

An archaeological site is essentially a man-made deposit which can be formed and reformed during its period of use in any number of ways. Domestic rubbish and materials used for building also play an important part in this process, and if a site is in use over a long period of time, quite deep deposits will often build up around areas in constant use. This is particularly true of settlements where the population increases steadily through time, and where there are either natural or even man-made obstacles to further expansion. By the 13th century, for example, the small island to the north of the original Hiberno-Viking settlement was reclaimed, settled and connected to the south island by a bridge. All of this area - the centre of the medieval city - was eventually enclosed with a defensive wall. Those who could afford to would have lived within its confines in order to avail of its protection and the various privileges granted to it.

Urban renewal, the replacement of old or derelict buildings with new ones within an urban area, is something which we tend to associate with our own era. But it was no less common in the medieval period, particularly when closely-spaced wooden houses with thatch roofs presented an ever-present fire hazard to all urban dwellers. In the event of a large-scale fire, there was often no choice other than to redevelop and rebuild. In Cork urban renewal generally resulted in the ground surface being raised upwards, when the demolished remains of older houses were levelled off to prepare the ground for new ones. Each period of redevelopment resulted in similar deposits being formed. Domestic rubbish either deliberately buried in pits or scattered outside the houses also contributed to this build-up of material, and in this way the remains of the medieval city became buried under later periods of urban development. The present level of the city streets, within the area corresponding to that enclosed by the city wall, had already been reached by the 18th century. Those who have taken the opportunity to visit any of the more recent excavations within the city will know that there is a substantial difference between present-day and medieval ground levels.

Of course, if all of these deposits were formed like a layer cake throughout the city, then the job of the urban archaeologist would be a relatively easy one. But as all areas were not necessarily developed or redeveloped at the same time, the build-up of deposits can not be expected to be uniform throughout. Thus the build up of deposits (or stratigraphic sequence) as revealed by an archaeological excavation in the north-west area of the medieval city might be quite different from what may be later found in the south-east. Thus, the excavations that have been conducted to-date can only present us with a partial picture of the city's development, though with time this is likely to become much clearer.

Yet there are other problems. The foundations of later buildings, especially those of the 18th and 19th centuries, are often dug into earlier archaeological deposits. Similarly, public services such as sewerage pipes and water mains can also present the archaeologist with many problems, particularly when the trenches laid out to receive them are deeply cut. The earliest archaeological deposits of the city are often seriously disturbed in this way, although those who will end up excavating them will have long been used to taking their archaeology as they find it. Indeed, there are no certainties where preservation is concerned. The daily rise and fall of the tide has ensured that the earliest levels of the city, along with any perishable materials such as wood, bone and leather associated with them, will be preserved if the material in which they have been deposited is continually waterlogged. But the extent to which this material may have been disturbed by later activity such as, for example, the sinking of a well, will not be known until an excavation is underway. Nonetheless, the overall conditions of preservation so far encountered in urban excavations in Cork have been excellent.

THE WALLED CITY

Nothing is currently known about the Viking and later Hiberno-Viking defences of Cork, save that they existed. However, it is likely that the

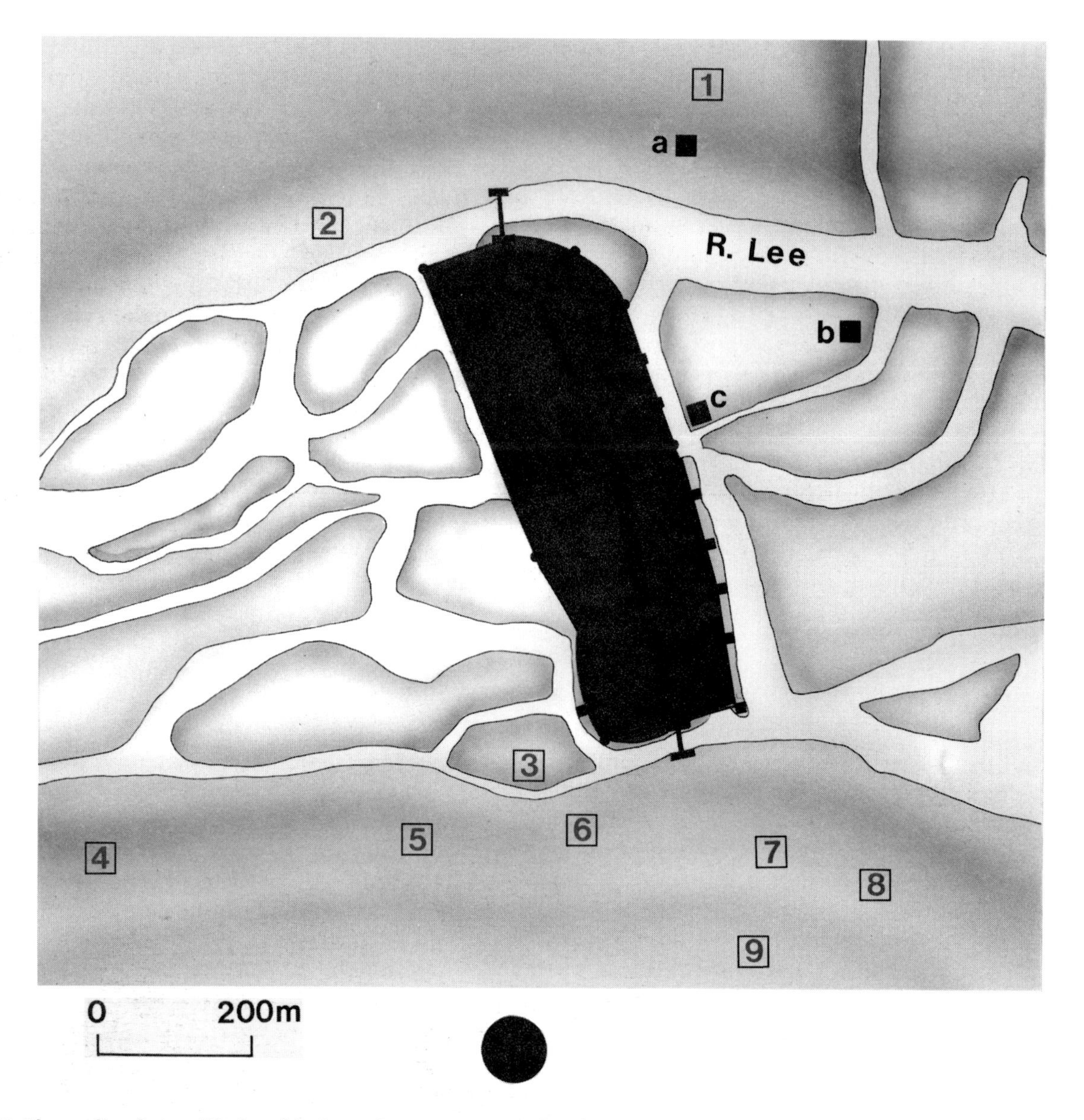

42. The medieval city of Cork and its immediate environs. ***1.*** *Church of St. Mary;* ***2.*** *Franciscan Friary;* ***3.*** *Dominican Priory;* ***4.*** *St. John The Evangelist – (Aug.);* ***5.*** *St. Finbarr's Cathedral;* ***6.*** *Church of St. Mary del Nard;* ***7.*** *Church of St. Nicholas;* ***8.*** *Augustnian Friary;* ***9.*** *Church of St. Brigid;* ***a.*** *Shandon Castle;* ***b.*** *Custum House House;* ***c.*** *Fort.*

Anglo -Normans used the Hiberno-Viking settlement as the nucleus of its own, which they later expanded to include the north island. By at least 1182 they had probably built a stone wall around the town, a task which they are likely to have immediately set about after their capture of the city five years earlier. According to 13th-century accounts the walled city was regularly flooded by the tidal movements of the River Lee, and we might expect that this seriously undermined the foundations of the wall. At any rate, large sums of money had been spent on the city walls by the beginning of the 14th century, although it is not known whether this involved the cost of repairing or extending them.

By the end of the 12th century the south island was connected to the north island (called Dungarvan) by a bridge; whilst a further bridge joined Dungarvan to the north bank of the River Lee. Dungarvan appears to have been a suburb of the city by the end of the 12th century, but it is not until the beginning of the 14th century that we find any indications that it was enclosed within the city walls. The inclusion of Dungarvan within the precincts of the city marks the greatest extent of the city walls. From time to time the documentary sources refer to repairs to the city walls, and in or around the year 1317 we even have some historical evidence to suggest that they were extensively rebuilt. This is not really surprising if we consider that during this period Cork was seen as an outpost of the Anglo-Norman colony, and that the maintenance of the wall would have been considered a priority. The upkeep of the walls was the responsibility of the citizens of Cork, but in difficult times payment was waived. The townspeople were still paying for their upkeep as late as the 17th century, but in the aftermath of the siege of 1690, they were no longer seen as a practical means of defending the city.

The walls of Cork would have enclosed an area of approximately 36 acres (about 14.5 hectares). Some 16 defensive towers were built along the walls to defend the city from all quarters, whilst access into the city precincts was controlled by two defended gates. The latter were built at opposite ends of the city's main thoroughfare. The North Gate commanded the bridge leading into the city from the suburb of Shandon on the north bank of the river, while its counterpart, the South Gate, defended the bridge leading to the south bank. Both of these bridges are likely to have originally been in the positions now occupied by the modern North and South Gate bridges. Two further openings in the walls were provided at the east and west: the Water Gate, near the Hanover Street area,

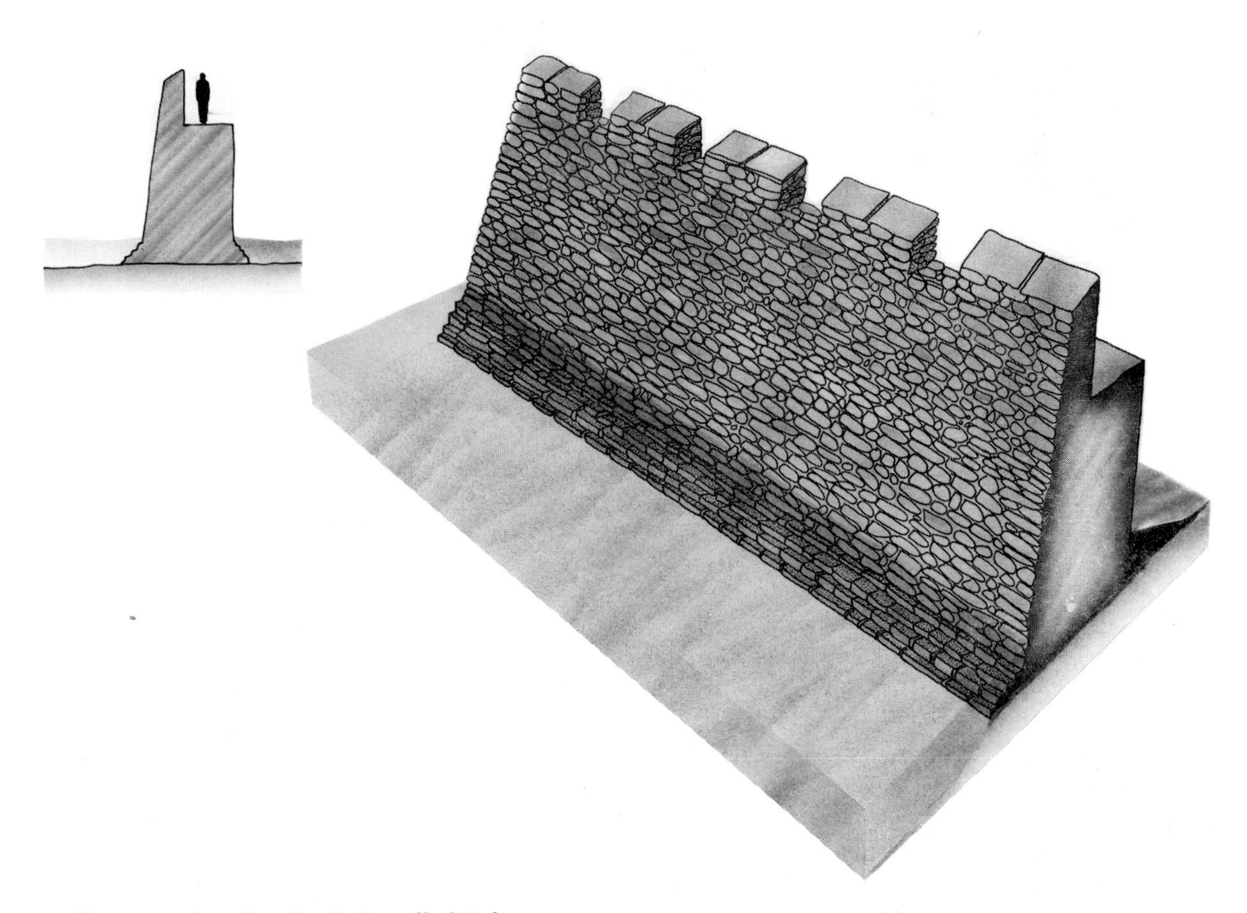

43. Reconstruction of medieval city wall of Cork.

44.Kyrl's Quay excavations, 1992. The exposed section of the city wall of Cork can be clearly seen on the right of the photograph.

and the Marine Gate near the eastern end of Castle Street. The Marine Gate enabled ships to sail into the city and discharge their cargoes in safety on the quayside. By at least 1206, and probably earlier, a stone castle had been built on the eastern city wall to defend this important entry point for shipping. This was later known as the King's Castle, and it would have stood roughly near the junction of Castle Street and the Grand Parade.

THE ARCHAEOLOGY OF CORK'S TOWN WALLS

Very little of the original city walls survives above pavement level, and only two of those which do are easily accessible. Two possible surviving sections of the wall are to be found behind the former Elmes Providers premises and the business premises numbers 2-4 on the east side of North Main Street. Neither of these are on public view, although two sections which came to light during archaeological excavations in the 1980s, on Grand Parade and Kifts Lane (inside the Grand Parade Hotel), are now on open display. A further incomplete section of wall also survives in the area between the northern end of Beamish and Crawford's brewery and the south side of Hanover Street

Limestone was the main building stone used in the city walls, but all of the excavated sections have shown that sandstone was often used in its facings (see below). The city of Cork has always been fortunate in having good quality limestone and sandstone close at hand. Indeed, there were large limestone outcrops on the south bank of the river near French's Quay, and further west of here at Gillabbey. It is likely that these were quarried throughout the medieval period, and when the walls were under construction boat loads of stone could have been shipped downstream to those areas in which wall foundations were being prepared.

45. Gateway in medieval city wall at Kyrl's Quay. The gateway was deliberately blocked-up sometime in the later medieval period

The sandstone used in the city walls, however, would have had to have been quarried on the north bank of the river.

The construction of the city walls must have been a difficult undertaking. Daily tidal flooding, and the inherently marshy nature of the islands upon which the city had been built, would have made the preparation of the foundations an onerous if not dangerous task. In most cases the foundations of the walls were laid directly upon river mud. But, even if the stone were unloaded from boats right next to the works, its haulage around this marshy area would have involved a lot of heavy labour. The section of medieval wall excavated at the junction of Tuckey Street and Grand Parade in 1980 had a "stepped" foundation, which was 4m wide at the base. The area upon which this wall's foundation was to be laid was first spread with a layer of moss and brushwood, and the large stone blocks making up the lowest step of the foundation were then laid directly on top of it. The moss and brushwood would have given the foundation a grip upon the underlying river mud, whilst the wide foundation of the wall helped to spread its weight more evenly. A layer of naturally deposited river gravel, beneath the mud upon which this section of wall had been built, also seems to have given it a reasonably sound foundation.

The inner and outer faces of the wall generally have a batter, which means that they taper upwards from the foundation. The stones which we see, the *facing* stones, are only an outer skin. The stones between the inner and outer faces of the walls are made up of tightly packed stone rubble, which is held together with mortar. There are, as we have seen, no complete sections of wall, but originally it would have been somewhere between 5 and 6m in height. The 16th-and 17th-century pictorial maps of the city also indicate that it had a stepped platform near the top for sentries called a wall walk, and that its parapet had crenellations. There also seem to have been stone steps at various points on the inner face of the wall to allow access to the wall walk. Very little is known about any of the 16 towers along the wall, but, in 1984, what appears to have been the base of the Hopewell tower came to light during the excavation of the section of wall now on full display in Bishop Lucey Park. A possible turret of the city wall was also investigated during the Cornmarket Street excavations of 1983.

In 1992 the longest section of city wall investigated to-date was excavated near Kyrl's Quay. Some 60m of wall was examined, most of which was 13th century in date, and which survived to a maximum height of around 3.2m. The wall also had two watergates – the first of their type to be excavated within the medieval city – through which small boats could be hauled down to or up from the river. One of these even had a paved slipway for drawing up boats, whilst the original wrought-iron hinge pivots also survived. There can thus be little doubt that this section of the wall also served as a quayside. The foundations of a mural tower also came to light during these excavations, the first to be fully investigated on the original line of the city wall. It was D-shaped in plan and its foundation was made up with dressed limestone blocks.

EVERYDAY LIFE WITHIN THE MEDIEVAL CITY

HOUSES AND STREETS

Medieval Cork had a main street which ran on a north-south axis through the centre of the walled town, the original line of which is today preserved in the North and South Main streets. A series of individually owned properties called *burgage plots* were laid out in narrow strips from the main street, and the boundaries between these are often preserved in the modern street pattern. Many of the narrow alleyways off North Main Street, for example, probably owe their origin to property boundaries laid out in the medieval period. Indeed, the remains of a medieval stone pathway off Cornmarket Street were investigated during excavations there in 1983. The Kyrl's Quay - North Main Street excavations clearly established continuity of property boundaries over at least eight hundred years. One alleyway leading from North Main Street, which had been set out in the late 13th or early 14th century, had been resurfaced many times until it finally fell into disuse in the 16th or 17th century. Excavations on the site of the College of the Holy Trinity off South Main Street in the early 1970s revealed clearly defined medieval property boundaries. These extended from South Main Street to the city wall on present day Grand Parade, in strips up to 25ft (7.62m) wide marked off with wickerwork fences, later replaced with stone walls. Post and wattle property boundaries also came to light during the Kyrl's Quay excavations. The Holy Trinity site has produced the best evidence for medieval houses of any of the Cork city sites excavated to-date. These includ-

46.Medieval property boundary as excavated at South Main Street in early 1970s. The wattle fence has been deliberately cut down to serve as a trackway

ed a series of well-preserved post-and-wattle (wickerwork) and timber-framed houses of the 12th and 13th centuries, some of which would have fronted onto the main street. Behind these were the remains of what appear to have been wooden sheds. The area between the city wall and these buildings, as was suggested by the Grattan Street and Holy Trinity excavations, appears to have been left open and may well have been used as garden plots or rubbish dumps.

The excavations at St Peter's Market, on Cornmarket Street, revealed the foundations of a late 13th / mid-14th century house with clay or mud walling. This particular house had a floor of brushwood and straw, a common feature of medieval houses where successive layers of such material became trampled into the ground through time, to be periodically replaced by new flooring material. House floors of compacted straw, dating to the mid-13th century, were also excavated near the Grand Parade section of the city wall. From at least the 13th century onwards stone houses began to gradually replace timber ones within the city. The houses excavated near the College of Holy Trinity appear to have followed this pattern, whilst at Grattan Street stone buildings were being constructed at a relatively early period in the development of the walled town. A similar pattern also emerged during the 1992 excavations on the east side of North Main Street, where 13th and 14th century timber-framed houses were later re-built in stone. Roofing slates recovered during the Cornmarket Street excavations also suggest that at least some of the houses in this general area must have had slate roofs.

Larger stone buildings have also been excavated, although these tend to be somewhat later. The remains of Skiddy's Castle, built by John Skiddy, bailiff and one time mayor of Cork in around 1443, were excavated at the north-western end of North Main Street in 1974. Most of this fortified town house was demolished in the late 18th century, but, as the excavations revealed, the building survived up to first-floor level. Its foundations were supported by an oak raft resting upon a series of vertical wooden piles, which had been rammed into the underlying peat. A large fragment of a mantle piece bearing the date 1597, and reputed to have come from Skiddy's Castle, can still be seen above the 3rd-floor window of No.13, North Main Street. The foundations of what would appear to have been a structure similar to Skiddy's Castle, almost directly opposite on the east side of North Main Street, were excavated in 1992. Holy Trinity Chantry College off South Main Street, founded by the rector of Holy Trinity, Philip Goold, in 1482, was excavated in 1975. This was a rectangular stone building 20m long, the foundation of which was set on wooden piles. Its side walls survived to a height of about 1m above the foundation course: again, as in the case of Skiddy's Castle, a remarkable survival.

AGRICULTURE

Up until the early 14th century supplies of wheat, oatmeal, malted barley, along with beef, pork and fish were exported from Cork for the English army in France. There can be little doubt that the city in this period had access to regular supplies of food, both for the needs of its inhabitants and for export. Like all towns, ancient and modern, Cork relied on the resources of the surrounding countryside for its food supply. By the end of the 14th century warfare and pestilence had caused serious interruptions to this supply, and the city suffered accordingly. It had become a costly colonial outpost, whose inhabitants had to be restrained from leaving by Royal decree. Towards the end of the 14th century it became necessary to import grain, with its citizens seeking and obtaining permission to have this brought by sea from the Dublin/Meath area.

Large quantities of animal bones and, more recently, the remains of cereal crops, have been recovered from medieval excavations in the city. Cattle, sheep, goat and pig appear to have been the main varieties of meat to grace the tables of medieval Cork. Indeed, the hides of cattle, horse, stag and goat, along with wool, also feature amongst the city's main exports during the medieval period. Animal produce such as wool and dairy products, along with by-products such as animal fat, hides for leather and bone for tools and ornaments, also figured promimently in the economy of the city and its environs. The horse bones which have turned up on the city excavations suggest that the animals involved were more like modern ponies, a suggestion which is largely confirmed by the size of the medieval horseshoes which have been found on at least two sites.

The Grattan Street excavations of 1990-91 have produced important evidence for the types of cereals eaten by the city's inhabitants during the medieval period. The remains of oats, hulled oats, bread wheat and spelt have all been identified in medieval deposits taken from this site. Yet, while all of these crops were probably grown within the environs of the city, it now seems clear that they were processed for eating within the city itself. The presence of oat chaff in the Grattan Street deposits suggests that this had been removed from the cereal grains when they were ground into meal. As this was the case, it would follow that the grain had been milled on-site. A similar picture, indeed, seems to be emerging from the medieval Waterford excavations. Medieval hand or rotary querns have been found on the Christchurch and Grattan Street sites, whilst the city was served by a number of water-powered mills within its immediate environs. As late as the early 17th century Fynes Moryson (1566-1630), secretary to Lord Deputy Mountjoy, felt obliged to comment upon the somewhat less than hygienic use of the rotary quern by "young maids" of Cork.

The seeds of a weed called corncockle, as recovered from the Grattan Street excavations, have provided us with a curious insight into the type of wheaten bread eaten in medieval Cork. Medieval farmers generally did not concern themselves with weeding, and this particular weed more often than not ended up being harvested and threshed with winter wheat. As corncockle seeds are quite heavy, it is impossible to separate them from cereal grains using traditional methods such as winnowing. However, they can be sorted and separated by hand, although this is an incredibly laborious process. In the event, the inhabitants of medieval Cork clearly chose not to do so, the end result being that the corncockle seeds would have been ground into the flour. At the very least this would have affected the taste of the bread, but at worst it may have been harmful to the health of the person eating it. Corncockle is a poisonous weed and, incredible though it must seem to us, the inhabitants of medieval Cork are likely to have been aware of this.

FISHING

From the earliest times the River Lee and the waters of Cork harbour have provided a bounteous supply of fish and shellfish for the people living along their shores. The former importance of the harbour's oyster fisheries is attested in the large number of shell middens or dumps, some of which still survive around the harbour's shoreline. Some 20 midden sites have been identified by the Cork Archaeological Survey within the harbour area, a good example of which can still be seen on the shoreline north of Curraghbinny Wood. A number of these may well prove to be prehistoric, but there is at least one example excavated near Carrigtohill which produced pottery of late 13th - early 14th century date. Enormous amounts of oyster shells have been recovered from medieval excavations conducted within the city, most recently at Grattan Street, where a substantial 13th-century midden had been formed up against a stone-walled building. Post-medieval middens have also been discovered within the environs of the city - most notably at the bottom of Sunday's Well Road - and the likelihood is that shellfish such as oysters, mussels, whelk and periwinkles formed an important part of the diet of the inhabitants of the city since its foundation.

The salmon fisheries of the River Lee were also fully exploited during the medieval period. Artefacts such as fish hooks and stone net-sinkers have turned up on city excavations, as have the bones of both fresh and salt water fish such as hake, herring and cod. We also have documentary evidence for the existence of fish weirs on the River Lee and its tributaries, such as the recently culverted Kiln River (near the present Christy Ring Bridge), from before the end of the 12th century. Indeed, nearly all of the important monasteries established near the city had fishing weirs on the Lee. The monastery of Gill Abbey, for example, had fisheries on the south channel, whilst the Dominicans controlled the main fishery on the north channel.

CRAFTS AND INDUSTRIES

Medieval craft-workshops, similar to those found in medieval Dublin, have yet to be found within the precincts of medieval Cork. There can be little doubt that workshops of craftsmen working in metal, bone, wood, leather and perhaps pottery, featured prominently within the commercial life of medieval Cork. The short sections which follow should serve to give the reader a good idea of the types of goods which are likely to have been manufactured within the city during the medieval period.

Metalworking: Sizeable quantities of iron slag and other residues of ironworking have been found during city excavations. These include the tell-tale, bowl-shaped, lumps of slag (furnace bottoms) which formed at the bottom of primitive furnaces during the iron-smelting process. We also have fragments of crucibles, the small ceramic bowls used for pouring molten metals into moulds, from the South Main Street and Grand Parade excavations. The range of medieval iron artefacts from the city excavations is a comprehensive one: single-edged knives, spearheads, nails and rivets; horse trappings such as horseshoes and horseshoe nails, snaffle bits and spurs; tools such as drill bits, shears, gouges and punches. Medieval barrel padlocks and keys have also been excavated, as have a number of large iron needles which may have been used in the manufacture of heavy-duty leather goods or even sailcloth. Thus far artefacts of bronze and lead have been less well represented. Bronze artefacts include stick pins (dress fasteners), buckles, needles and keys, along with more spectacular items such as the remarkable 13th-century bronze candlestick with folding legs from the Grand Parade excavations, currently in Cork Public Museum. A number of lead items, which include some possible lead weights, have also come to light, and there is also a pewter token from Christchurch Place.

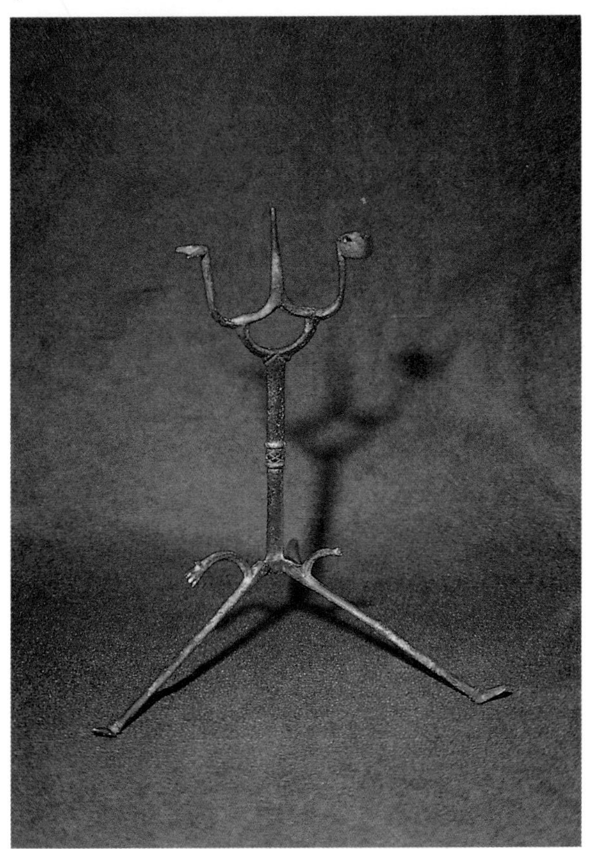

47. Thirteenth-century bronze candlestick holder with folding legs, from Grand Parade excavations, Cork city.

Bone Artefacts: Deer antler was an important raw material in the manufacture of many everyday items such as combs: about 95% of the medieval combs found on Cork city excavations were made from it. Antler gaming pieces such as chessmen and dice are also relatively common, and at least one wooden board for a game called "nine mens' morris" has been found in the city. Generally speaking, antler which was not of the quality required for comb making appears to have been used for making gaming pieces. Deer are likely to have been hunted in the wooded areas within the immediate environs of the city and beyond, and deer antler is likely to have been a commodity regularly traded within the city. Bone net braiding needles, spindle whorls, bobbins and reels, and even toggles similar to those used on latter day "duffle" coats have also been found. An inscribed, highly polished, bone seal matrix (a badge of office), dating to the 13th century, was discovered during the Grand Parade excavations. The same excavation also yielded up the remains of a bone whistle, while the South Main Street excavations produced a medieval

48. Medieval bone gaming pieces from Cork city excavations.

bone harp peg. In the medieval period wooden caskets, decorated with strips of bone, were often used to hold valuables. Bone strips which are likely to have served this purpose have also been found in Cork.

Wood: A wide variety of wooden artefacts have been recovered during city excavations, which include everything from wooden spoons to tuning pegs for musical instruments. Most of the spoons, incidentally, were made from yew, a wood which may not have left a pleasant taste on the tongue. It seems likely, therefore, that these spoons were for stirring or mixing food rather than for eating with. Impressive lathe-turned bowls, made from woods like ash and alder (but also of birch and hazel), have also been found as have the remains of stave built vessels.

Leather: The remains of three leather shoes (which included at least one man's shoe and one woman's shoe) were discovered during the city wall excavations on Grand Parade in 1980. One of these retained its thong, or leather shoe lace. Over 500 pieces of leather (mostly of shoes) were excavated on the second main Grand Parade wall excavation in 1985, which also included decorated leather knife sheaths. Both knife and sword sheaths were also recovered during the South Main street excavations of 1975.

Pottery: Enormous quantities of fragmented medieval pottery vessels from Cork city excavations have been found over the last two decades, but only a small amount of it was made in Ireland. Very little is known about native pottery. We have yet to find a medieval Irish pottery kiln, and consequently our knowledge of the techniques used by the native potter during this period is somewhat limited. Nonetheless, some of the native medieval pottery from Cork is different from that generally found on medieval sites in south Leinster. As only a small amount of the south Leinster pottery has been found in Cork, there is a strong possibility that the other Irish-made pottery may have been made locally.

Textiles: Woollen cloth was exported from Cork during this period, and there can be little doubt that woollen yarn was spun and woven within the city. Three pieces of woven woollen

49. *Medieval wooden spoons and lathe-turned bowl from Cork city excavations.*

50. Sixteenth-century Bellarmine jar from Cork city excavations.

cloth were recovered during the Grand Parade excavations of 1985. A careful analysis of these showed that red and yellow dyes had been used to colour them, although it was not altogether clear what type of garments they originally formed part of. Nonetheless, a number of hairs which had been caught on the surface of the fabric were human, and apparently came from a dark-haired person.

FOREIGN TRADE

In the later medieval period the English army at Gascony and Bayonne was partly provisioned by ships from Cork. Documentary sources tell us that these ships carried cargoes of meat, cereals and malt, and that on their return to Cork they would have brought with them wine, English and French cloth, spices, vegetables and kitchen utensils. Bordeaux, Calais and Dieppe are the main French ports which are mentioned, whilst the main English ports of call appear to have been Bristol, Carlisle, Pembroke, Portsmouth and Southampton. The hides of small animals such as foxes, squirrels and martens, along with perhaps some live meat (in addition to the commodities listed above) and woollen goods, were amongst Cork's contributions to international trade in this period.

Archaeology has also played an important role in establishing the extent of Cork's foreign trade in this period. Many different types of French and English medieval pottery vessels have been found on Cork city excavations, and these provide us with a good indication of the

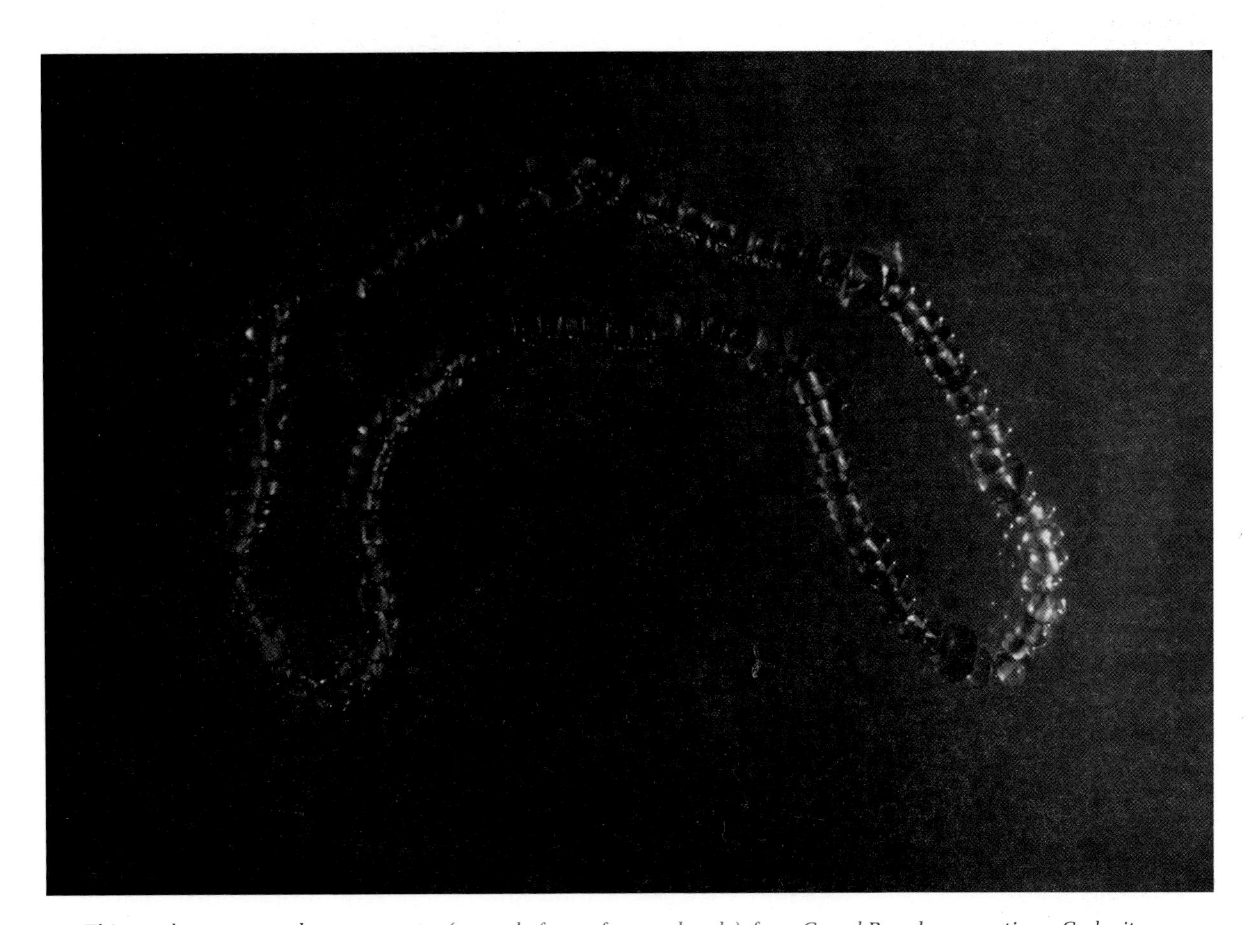

51. Thirteenth-century amber paternoster (an early form of rosary beads), from Grand Parade excavations, Cork city.

places medieval Cork was trading with. The main type of medieval French pottery which has been found in Cork comes from the Saintonge region of south-western France, though medieval pottery from the Paris-Caen region, and a distinctive red-painted ware from Normandy, have also turned up on city excavations. The main variety of English medieval pottery found within the medieval city comes from Ham Green near Bristol, but there is also pottery from other English regions such as Scarborough and West Wiltshire. The changing patterns of Cork's foreign trade continued to be reflected in the type of pottery imported into the city in the post-medieval period. Typical of these would be North Devon wares, fine German wares from Bellarmine and Westerwald and occasional Spanish wine jars.

One of the most exciting discoveries in recent years is the late 13th-century amber paternoster found during the Grand Parade excavations of 1985. As we have already seen amber, a product of Scandinavian forests, was imported into Ireland from the prehistoric period onwards. The Cork paternoster - an early form of rosary beads - was made up of 88 small beads and 10 larger ones. It was almost certainly a luxury item (its original owner can hardly have been too pleased about losing it), and may well have been manufactured by a craftsman within the city itself.

THE ARCHAEOLOGY OF THE CHURCH

The medieval city of Cork and its immediate environs was well provided with churches and monastic foundations, but only a small number of sites and architectural features and fragments associated with these have survived. There is only one standing later medieval church building, part of Red Abbey (see below), which has survived later urban development within the city. Yet as early as the 18th century, many of the surviving remains of many of the city and general harbour area's medieval churches and monasteries had already been demolished. And so while it is possible to plot the positions of all of these on distribution maps, we know very little about their physical appearance.

52. Red Abbey, Cork, an Augustinian foundation.

The chapter house door of the Dominican Priory of St. Mary (the "abbey of the isle"), has been incorporated into the present St. Finbarr's cathedral. St Mary's was founded by Philip de Barry (a nephew of Robert Fitzstephen) in 1229, on the small island to the southwest of the walled city. There is a 14th-century ivory figurine of the virgin and child, which probably

53. Later medieval slit-light window at Ballynacorra Church, County Cork.

belonged to the Abbey of the Isle, in the present-day Dominican house on Pope's Quay. The figurine is said to have been brought to Ireland by a former Bishop of Cashel, Maurice O'Carroll, in 1304. In 1988 a small test excavation was carried out on the northern section of the abbey island. The preliminary results of this excavation suggest that the area outside the precincts of the abbey was occupied as early as the 13th century, and perhaps earlier. This is the first area outside the walled city to produce evidence for medieval occupation.

The Augustinian order became established in Cork sometime in the late 13th century, on a site outside the city walls near present day Douglas Street. All that survives of this foundation is a 15th century four-storey tower, which originally would have been at the centre of a cruciform (i.e. cross-shaped) building. The eastern "arm" of this building would have been taken up by the nave (the main body of the church) and the western arm by the chancel (the area containing the altar). The areas to the north and south of the tower would also have had low transepts or arms.

Holy Trinity Church on South Main Street (Christchurch), may well have been the principal church of the Hiberno-Norse settlement at Cork. The present church was built in the early 1720s, and replaced a medieval church on the same site. Indeed, part of the current church's crypt, which contains a 13th century stone effigy, may have formed part of the original medieval church.

A number of later-medieval parish churches have survived within the harbour area, the best examples of which are at Carrigtohill, Ballynacorra and Churchtown. The later-medieval parish church of Carrigtohill (which appears to have been associated with Barryscourt Castle, the seat of the Barry family (see below, Chapter 4), is larger than the usual parish church of this period. The remains of its nave and chancel survive, along with an impressive rectangular, four-storey tower which appears to be of later-medieval date. The medieval church at Ballynacorra which, while showing signs of repair and presently very overgrown, does retain a number of its original ogee-headed windows. Churchtown Church –

54. Aumbry and piscina in later medieval church at Churchtown, Co. Cork

the later medieval parish church of Inchinabracky - also retains some interesting medieval features, which include an *aumbry* (a recess beside the altar to hold the sacred vessels) and a *piscina* (a recess which held a stone water bowl, in which the priest washed his hands).

FOUR

Castles and Artillery Fortifications

Many of the early castles within the Cork harbour area were designed for local warfare, which was generally sporadic and often inconclusive. Most attacks on tower houses were seldom long enough to be dignified with the term "siege", and more often than not their owners had only to hold out against raiding parties. The realities of warfare in later medieval Ireland were such that the elaborate siege warfare waged in early Renaissance Italy, with the help of professional military engineers, was not a threat with which Irish chieftains had to contend. Gunpowder artillery, indeed, was not used in Ireland until the late 15th century, by which time it had already revolutionised warfare throughout Europe. But in Ireland tower houses continued to be built, in the knowledge that one's local enemies were unlikely to call with cannon in tow.

However, the development of shipborne cannon and its increased use from the 15th century onwards, brought a new threat to coastal defences and a need for existing coastal fortifications to be able to respond in kind. In this regard the defences of both Cork city and harbour were to be found wanting. The city of Cork was considered to be one of the most poorly defended within the kingdom of Great Britain, although the natural headlands at the harbour mouth did have great potential, which a succession of British military engineers began to exploit from the early 17th century onwards.

The expansion of the port of Cork in the 18th century, and its increased importance in British transatlantic communications and trade, brought with it the added burden of its defence. Cork harbour became the main British naval base in Ireland, and the development of its coastal defences throughout the 18th and 19th centuries (often fuelled by successive French invasion scares) is a reflection of its strategic importance within the former British empire. The British naval presence in Cork harbour led to its development as one of the most heavily-defended ports in the realm, whilst Corkmen served in many capacities throughout the British navy, whose ranks were swelled by substantial numbers of Irishmen by the end of the 18th century.

TOWER HOUSES

The vast majority of surviving castles within the harbour area are tower houses, a type of fortification which became common throughout Ireland during the 15th century, when centralised authority had all but broken down. They were a simple expedient, whose origins in Ireland may well date to the beginning of the 14th century. More conventional castles with elaborate defences would have been beyond the means of many, but the tower house offered a relatively cheap alternative to those for whom holding out against a local raiding party was a more likely threat than a full-blown siege. Tower houses normally consist of a square or rectangular central tower, up to four stories high, surrounded by an enclosure called a bawn. The best surviving example of a stone *bawn* wall within the harbour area is at Barryscourt Castle near Carrigtohill, but in certain instances the bawn could also have been formed with wattles or even hedges. In most cases the roof of the ground floor is vaulted to protect the upper floors from fire, and when the plaster work covering the outer faces of the vault crumbles away the wicker work used in its construction is often revealed.

The most imposing tower house within the harbour area is Barryscourt Castle, strategically located near what would have been the main road between the important medieval ports of Cork and Youghal, and the *Bohur-na-bo-ruadh* - an early medieval routeway linking Glanmire with the monastic town of Cloyne. Early in the 19th century the land to the south and west of the castle was still covered by high tides, and it appears that the castle could have originally been approached by boat. The tower house is rectangular in plan and is partly enclosed by an impressive bawn wall which has towers at its south-east, north- east and north-west corners. The fields to the north and west of the surviving buildings bear traces of what may have originally been a defensive ditch or fosse.

Barryscourt Castle has three main floors: a ground floor level with an impressive six-metre wide vault over it, a first floor and a Great Hall at third-floor level. The main tower block, which is gabled, has three projecting towers which housed private chambers, storage and administrative areas, latrines, a chapel and a dungeon. The earliest parts of the castle complex possibly date to the 13th and 14th centuries, the bawn wall and its corner towers are likely to have been erected in the 15th century. As for the present tower house, it seems that it originally was a simple, rectangular structure, with the projecting towers added at a later date. During the Desmond rebellion of 1581 the castle was said to have been "defaced and despoiled" and was later briefly used as a residence by Sir Walter Raleigh. However, for the greater part of its history it was the baronial centre of Barrymore, and its role as the main residence of the Barry family only ended with the death of David Barry in 1617. Thereafter, the Barry family's principal residence became established at Castlelyons.

On the north shore of Great Island, commanding an important fording point, is the four-storey Belvelly Castle. Up until 1807, when the adjacent road bridge was constructed, this was the only access point to the island, and there can be little doubt that this site was carefully chosen. Belvelly Castle is in quite good condition and, in terms of the surviving stonework, really only lacks its battlements. It is rectangular in plan and has an impressive wicker-centred vault. The tower also has a "murder hole" - an aperture in the floor over the entrance lobby - which enabled the castle's defenders to dispatch anyone daring enough to attempt to force an entry through the main entrance chamber. Belvelly Castle is likely to be a 15th-century structure built by the Hodnett family, although the surviving coat of arms on the ground floor is possibly that of Sir Peter Courthope, who is known to have occupied the castle in the first half of the 16th century. There is also a somewhat smaller, four-storey tower house on the northern shoreline of Great Island, known as Ballymacshanroe Castle, which is 6.8m by 5.4m in extent and has a wicker-centred arch.

Cahermone Castle, which overlooks the Dungourney River, survives as an imposing four-storey tower house, but when originally built it is likely to have been even higher. A murder hole commands the first floor doorway, and other important surviving features are a garderobe or latrine chamber and a fireplace on

55. General view of Barryscourt Castle, near Carrigtohill, Co. Cork.

the east wall which has a tall chimney stack. The initials of John Fitz-Edmond, along with the date "1579", are inscribed on what appears to be the archstone from the castle's doorway, which survives in a nearby farmyard. Of particular interest are a number of gun loops, a feature rare in Cork harbour tower houses, which were designed for discharging firearms. Indeed, many Irish tower houses were built in a period when Italian engineers were beginning to design fortifications which could sustain attack by artillery. And while Irish tower houses made no pretense at being able to do so, a number did eventually incorporate features such as gun loops to take into account the use of firearms by the defenders.

Overlooking Lough Beg and the harbour are the remains of Barnahely Castle, a tower house with a surviving section of bawn wall, which has a single surviving gun loop. At ground floor level there is a poorly preserved fireplace, and two others at first floor level. The castle itself was built by the de Cogan family in 1536, and was occupied by them up until 1642 when the castle was surrendered to Murrough O'Brien, Lord Inchiquin, after being subjected to an attack with ordnance. Carrigaline Castle, on the north shore of the Owenboy estuary, occupies the site of an important de Cogan castle, which was built in the 13th century. The surviving remains on this site, however, are likely to have been part of a later Fitzgerald castle. As we have seen in Chapter 3 there are no surviving tower houses within the city of Cork. The nearest surviving example within its environs is in fact Dundanion Castle, which has three stories.

56.Chapel at Great Hall level, Barryscourt Castle. The wicker centering for the vault is clearly visible over the chapel window.

57. Belvelly Castle, Great Island.

The corbels, the projecting stones which supported original wooden floors, are clearly visible within the structure, which has fireplaces on the first and second floors. Dundanion Castle appears to have been built by the Galway family sometime before 1564.

EARLY ARTILLERY FORTIFICATIONS

The use of canon in sieges in Ireland is a late 15th-century development. In spite of this, tower houses continued to be built as late as the 17th century, although with new features such as gun loops which gave due recognition to the increasing use of hand guns in ordinary warfare. However, the relative austerity of the tower house was beginning to be replaced by the relative comfort associated with houses of the Tudor period. In Ireland the type of aristocratic country house which flourished in England during the Tudor and Stewart periods could not be introduced without some provision for defence. Thus, in Ireland, while fortified houses were clearly designed with a view to the increased comfort of their owners, distinctive features such as corners towers with musket loops, mark them off from similar English houses of the same period.

Monkstown Castle, built by the Old English Archdekin family in 1636, is an excellent example of this type of fortified house. It consists of a central, three-storey, rectangular block with a series of projecting four-storey towers at each corner. Each of the towers has a bartizan, a projecting turret, which enabled defenders to provide extra covering or flanking fire. The ground floor, where potential attackers would be most likely to attempt a forced entry, was provided with about twenty-five gun loops, many of which have subsequently been blocked up. Monkstown Castle is very similar to Mount Long at Oyster Haven and it is thought that both houses were built by the same architect. Currently abandoned, Monkstown Castle was

58. Barnahely Castle, Co. Cork.

used as a British army barracks in the 19th century and as a clubhouse for Monkstown Golf Club between 1908-71.

From the middle of the 16th century onwards an entirely new variety of fortification, specifically designed to withstand attacks by artillery, began to be built throughout Europe. The distinctive star-shaped plan of many of these forts derived from the use of four-sided angle bastions, which were designed to provide flanking fire and to position artillery pieces. Defences began to be developed in layers emanating outwards from the curtain wall, in such a way that potential attackers could be kept under fire for as long as possible by the defenders. Angle bastions - spear-shaped projections constructed at all of the enclosing walls' main corners - enabled the fort's garrison to pin down an attacking force in a crucial 100ft-wide area immediately in front of the curtain wall. Furthermore, the positioning of batteries on each bastion enabled the garrison to return artillery fire.

During the late 16th century work began on a fortification which was later known as King John's Fort on the east side of the harbour, near the latter day Carlisle Fort. In or around 1582 a circular artillery fortification, now incorporated into the present-day Blackrock Castle on the south bank of the River Lee, was built to cover the river approaches to the city. The Blackrock artillery tower appears to have been a local initiative designed to ward off casual raiders. It has five even-spaced embrasures for cannon around its circumference, which could originally have commanded extensive fields of fire. Its more recent additions were designed by the Pain brothers and built between the years 1828-29. In more recent times a magnificent fireplace dated 1627, originally from Ronayn's Court near Rochestown, has been installed on the ground floor of the tower. However, it was only in the aftermath of the defeat of the Spanish at Kinsale, in 1601, that the defence of the city and harbour from seaborne attack began to be viewed with any urgency.

In the early 1600s Lord Mountjoy, the English Lord Deputy, laid the foundations for the defence of the harbour. Mountjoy was fortunate enough to have on his staff a military engineer called Paul Ive - the first English engineer to write and publish a treatise on fortification - who had acquired considerable experience in the Low Countries. Ive, who was reponsible for the re-fortification of Pendennis Castle at Falmouth and for military works in the Channel Islands, was put to work on the construction of star-shaped forts on Haulbowline Island in 1602 and what was to become James Fort at Kinsale. Ive was to die at Kinsale before either work could be completed. Nonetheless, Sir George Carew, the President of Munster, was able to garrison the new bastioned fort at Haulbowline in 1602, and work on the fort was eventually completed under the direction of Samuel Molyneux in 1604. In 1624 the Haulbowline fort was described as "a very strong fort standing on an island, the walls being made of sod-

59.Dundanion Castle, Mahon peninsula.

60. Fireplace at Dundanion Castle.

61. Monkstown Castle, Cork, a seventeenth-century fortified house.

62. Blackrock Castle, Co. Cork, showing original artillery tower with gun embrasure still visible.

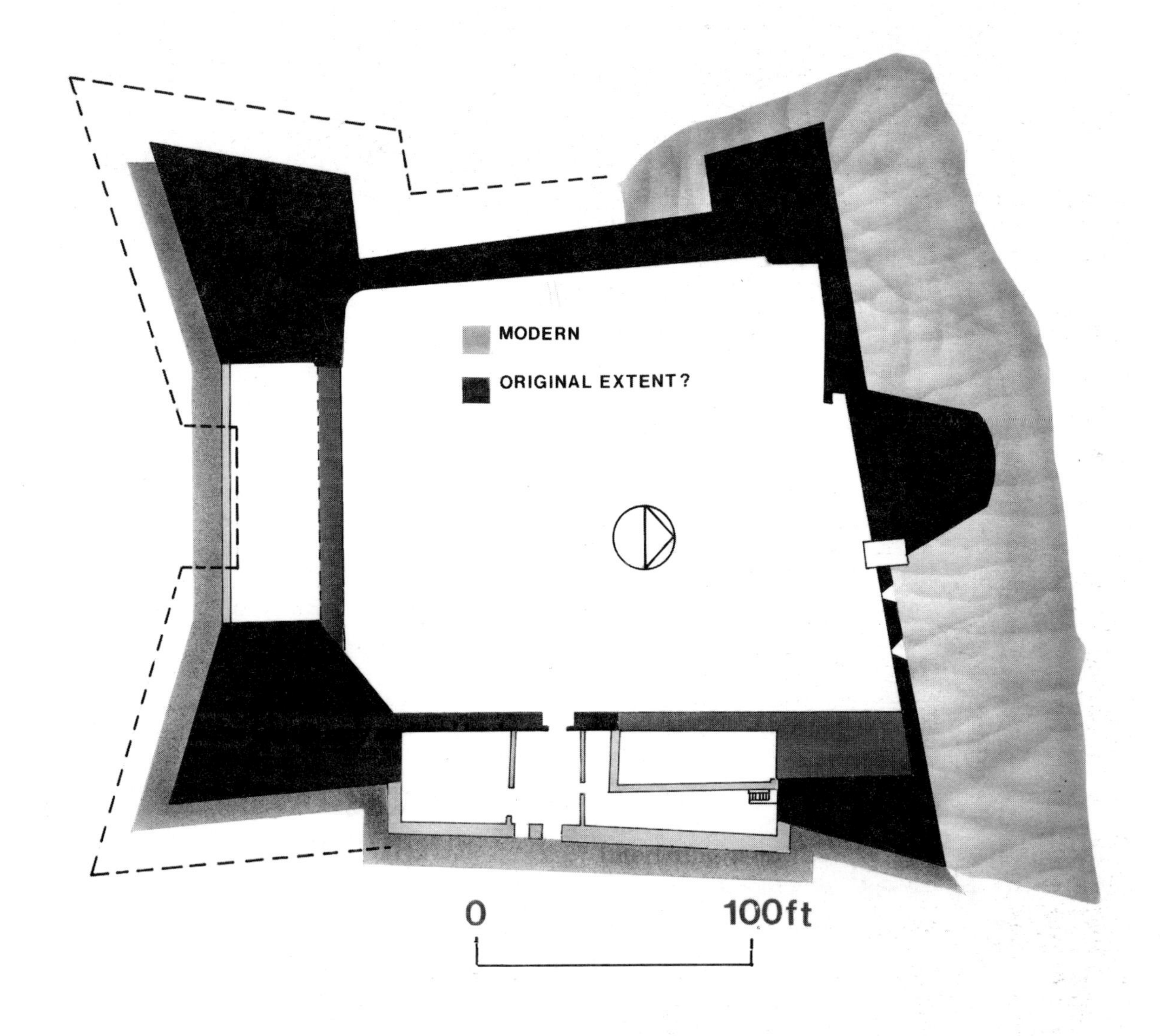

63. Ground plan of Elizabeth Fort, Cork city.

des and earth." Its curtain wall and the south-east bastion still survive.

At the turn of the 17th century Sir George Carew declared that Cork was "one of the weakest places to be defended from an enemy" that he had ever seen. Indeed, the increasing use of cannon in siege warfare exposed glaring weaknesses in the city of Cork's essentially medieval defenses against artillery attack. The islands upon which the city was built along with the walls constructed to enclose them, may well have provided a large measure of protection against a medieval army. But, in the age of gunpowder, the hills to the north and south of the city provided excellent artillery positions from which a determined attacker could bombard the town. Carew proposed that a fort be built at Cork "to bridle the town". While the bastioned fort at Haulbowline was under construction, he arranged for an "irregular work" of earth and timber to be thrown up on the south side of the city, which served as the nucleus for what later became Elizabeth Fort. The work was reluctantly carried out by the citizens of Cork who later destroyed it as a protest against the accession of James I and took its guns within the city walls. However, Lord Mountjoy was able to procure a surrender of the city and its citizens were obliged to rebuild the fort. In or around 1624 the fort was replaced with a more regular structure, to which a number of additions were made throughout the 17th century.

After the siege of 1690, during which Elizabeth Fort was taken without a major struggle, the fort itself had more or less ceased to be an effective means of defending the city. The fort's further expansion had effectively been checked by the build-up of domestic dwellings in the streets to the south of it, and a new barrack was built nearby in 1698. In 1719 a barrack for 700 men was built within the precincts of the fort, and it appears that by this period parts of its ramparts had been removed to make more space. It currently houses Barrack Street Garda Station, but during the 19th century it had at one time accommodated a female prison.

The fort was built on a limestone precipice overlooking the south wall of the city, at an elevation of about 18m above sea level. Two angle bastions face the south of the city, projecting outwards into present-day Fort Street, whilst two demi (i.e two-sided) bastions and a flat bastion face northwards over present-day Proby's Quay. A rock-cut ditch is also likely to have been in place around the southern walls of the fort, although this has long since been filled in.

THE 18TH CENTURY AND THE NAPOLEONIC WARS.

By the end of the 18th century Cork harbour had become the lynch-pin of British naval operations in Ireland. The lower harbour at Cork could easily accommodate the largest naval squadron or transatlantic convoy, and naval facilities became increasingly concentrated here, whilst the port itself became the seat of the Admiralty's victualling agent in Ireland. Indeed, the port of Cork's pre-eminence in the Irish provision trade eventually led to the accreditation of both Spanish and Portuguese consular officials to Cork. The strategic significance of the harbour in terms of transatlantic shipping and the defence of the western approaches was not lost on the British, who

64. Early eighteenth-century artillery fort at Carrignafoy, Great Island.

65. Arched doorway at Carrignafoy fort, Great Island.

were almost continually at war with the French from the 1750s up until the end of the Napoleonic Wars. Between 1743 and 1749 a roughly star-shaped fort was built to the east of Cobh at Carrignafoy, overlooking the harbour entrance. From the outset it was equipped with some twenty artillery pieces facing out into the harbour. In 1804 it had three batteries, a low level battery with six 24-pounder guns, 13 on the middle level battery and a single 24-pounder on the upper level battery. The surviving bastions are all equipped with musket loops. A second star-shaped fort was built to strengthen the harbour defences on Spike Island at the end of the 18th century. A battery of twenty-one 24 pounders had been erected on the island in 1779, but at the end of the American Wars in 1783 this was abandoned. Work on the new fort began in 1790 under the direction of General Charles Vallancey and the Cork architect Michael Shanahan, who had built the first St Patrick's Bridge. What later became known as Fort Westmorland (and later still as Dun an Mhistealaigh) was hexagonal in plan, with bastion faces about 46m long with flanks around 30m long; the fort itself being the apex in a triangle formed with Forts Carlisle and Camden which commanded the entrance to the harbour (see below). The fort was used between 1847 and 1883 as a prison, which up until 1856 housed political prisoners awaiting transportation, its most famous transportee being the Fenian John Mitchel.

In 1803 Britain faced a very real threat from invasion by France, a threat which brought about a complete overhaul of Britain's coastal defences. The French landings in Ireland during the 1798 rebellion and Robert Emmett's rebellion of 1803, which coincided with the French build-up along the coastline facing Britain across the English Channel, heightened British fears of further French attempts to invade Ireland. In the early 1790s the temporary defences at the mouth of Cork harbour were strengthened and established on a more permanent basis, although the design of the new fortifications was by no means state of the art. However, full advantage was taken of the rela-

66. Aerial view of Belvelly Martello tower, Great Island, showing how tower commands access across Belvelly bridge. Belvelly Castle (see fig. 57 above) can be seen to the right of the photograph.

67. Rossleague Martello tower, Great Island.

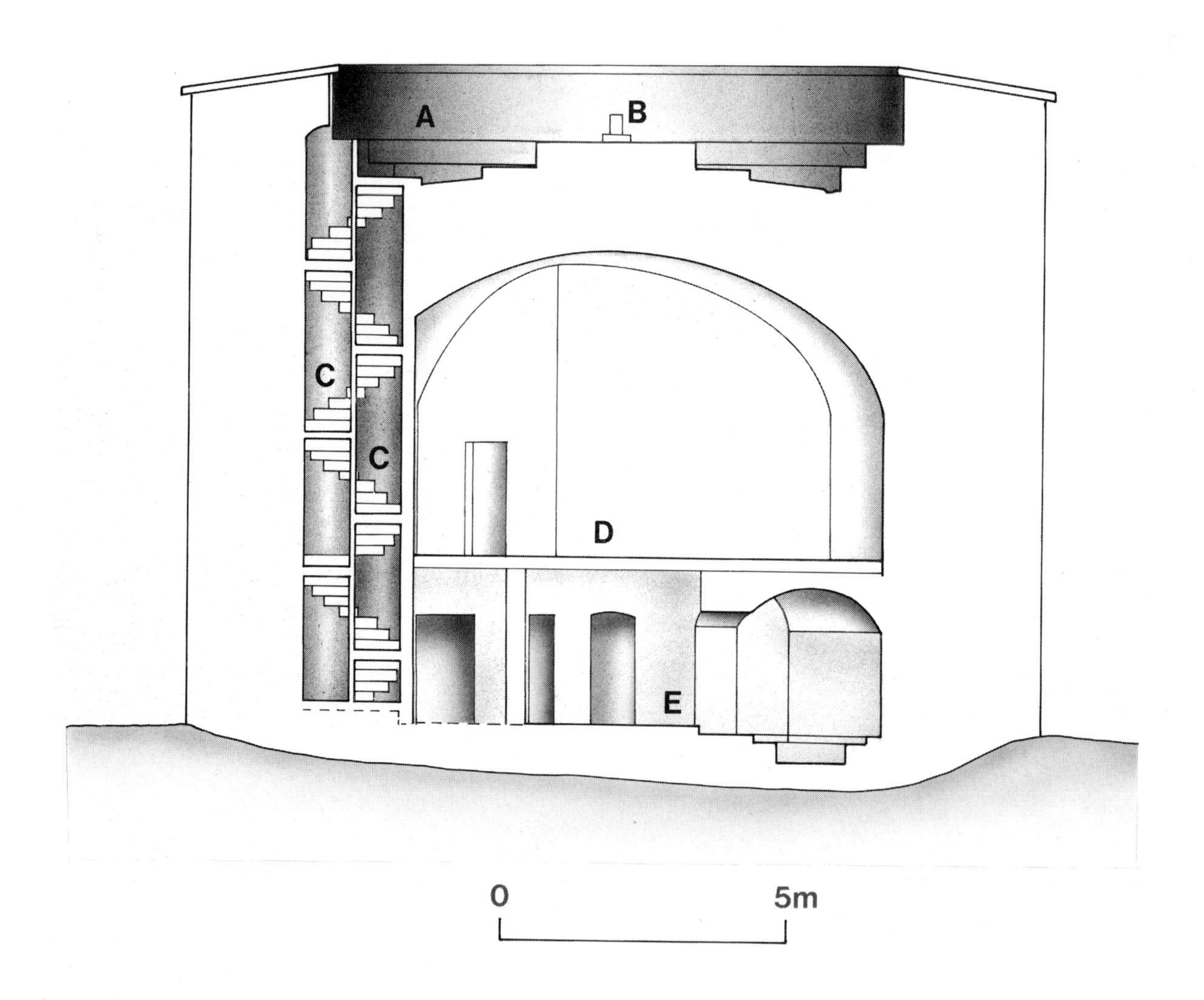

68. Section through Rossleague Martello tower: (a) gun platform, (b) pivot for traversing gun carriage, (c) spiral staircase to all levels, (d) living quarters for garrison, (e) stores and magazine.

tive narrowness of the harbour mouth, each side of which had cliff top eminences on which coastal batteries could be constructed.

Some provision for a coastal battery on the eastern side of the harbour entrance was already in place by the end of the 16th century. By 1685 there were two structures here, King John's Fort and a building to the south of it enclosed by a square defence work with an east-facing bastion, called Prince Rupert's Tower. Prince Rupert is clearly Rupert of Palatinate, a cousin of Charles I and later a fleet commander

69. Pivot for traversing gun carriage for 24-pounder gun as it survives on Rossleague Martello tower.

of Charles II, and the structure which bears his name was probably constructed in the 1640s. The battery is generally held to have fired upon the Duke of Marlborough's forces as they entered the harbour in 1690, but it now seems more likely that they came under fire from a temporary battery on the western side of the harbour entrance. Rupert's tower is shown on a plan of about 1701, where it is called "Corkbeg Fort", and is shown with a seaward facing battery with six gun embrasures. In 1780 the fort was named Carlisle Fort after the 5th Earl of Carlisle, and shortly after 1793 was made a permanent feature of the harbour defences. The cliff upon which the fort is located is at an elevation of 61m, and the fort itself was constructed in the form of an east-facing bastion which was flanked on each side by demi-bastions. The garrison was thus defended against landward attack, the actual coastal batteries being positioned in detached gun emplacements, set at irregular intervals along the hillside. A number of these emplacements had shot furnaces for producing red-hot shot which, after impacting against wooden ships, could also induce fires. Some fifty-three guns were positioned here in 1804, most of which were 24-pounders.

The opposite side of the harbour entrance was commanded by Fort Camden which, during the American war, was known as Ram's Head Fort after the adjacent headland. The site on Crosshaven Hill appears to have been fortified since the 1550s. In or around 1600 additions were made to the early works, but in the aftermath of the defeat of the Irish rebels and their Spanish allies at Kinsale in 1601, they appear to have been abandoned. A battery consisting of two blockhouses and eight pieces of ordnance was established on the site by Jacobite forces, and "James' Battery" opened up upon the Williamite fleet as it entered the harbour in 1690. The fort was rebuilt in the 1790s with a formidable rock-cut ditch with a rampart of tenaille trace, a special form of defensive outwork made up of redans (two banks forming an open-ended triangle or salient angle) set at right-angles to one another to make a zig-zag front. As at Fort Carlisle the batteries trained on the harbour entrance were arranged in detached emplacements down the hillside. Fort Camden (which was named after the Earl of Camden, John Pratt, Lord Lieutenant of Ireland 1795-98) was equipped with thirteen 24-pounders in 1804.

MARTELLO TOWERS

The immediate British response to the threat of a French invasion in the early 1800s was an ambitious scheme to improve the beach defences at key locations throughout Britain and Ireland. And the net result of this strategy was the construction of a large number of independent gun towers, capable of both firing upon hostile naval vessels and holding out against sustained attack from shipborne ordnance. Two important developments led to the decision to build these gun towers, commonly referred to as Martello towers. Some twenty years earlier similar towers had been built to defend the Channel Islands, whilst a similar type of gun tower at Cape Mortella in Corsica had put up an impressive fight against a British naval squadron in 1794. Mortella ("myrtle") soon gained an "o", and thus transformed the term Martello entered the English language. The majority of the Martello towers on the English coastline were built between 1805 and 1812. The Dublin bay Martellos, built in 1804, thus belong to the first phase of construction, but as we shall now see the Cork Harbour Martellos were erected rather late in the sequence.

Five Martellos were built in Cork harbour between 1813 and 1815, on Haulbowline Island, at Monning, Belvelly and Rossleague on Great Island and at Ringaskiddy. The Cork harbour Martellos differ from those built in Dublin Bay, in that they have vertical enclosing walls (the Dublin examples are shaped like up-turned flower pots), eliptical ground plans and larger overall diameters. As in the case of the Belvelly Martello which, like the adjacent tower house, had been built to cover an important access point to Great Island, the Cork harbour Martellos were erected at strategically important locations.

The Cork harbour Martellos are mainly eliptical in plan, with walls of cut, local limestone up to 2.5m thick. Access was generally at first floor level via a moveable ladder, although at Ringaskiddy, the largest example in the harbour area, the ditch surrounding the tower suggests that primary access to the site was by means of a drawbridge. This was a common practice at English sites where the tower was in a very exposed position. The ground floor was taken up by the magazine, general stores and water storage cisterns. Indeed, the garrison's need to be wholly independent in terms of its water supply occasionally led to a deep well being sunk inside the tower as at Rossleague. The first floor, access to which was gained through a trap-door, would have been divided up into separate living quarters for up to twenty four men and one officer. The original wooden floor and trap-door of the Rossleague Martello actually survive *in situ*. The roof of the tower, carried on a brick vault, was flat and entirely surrounded by a parapet, from which the tower's chimneys and ventilation shafts emerged. The flat-topped roof also served as a platform for the 24-pounder gun, which pivotted on a special traversing carriage, enabling the gunners to rotate the cannon through three-hundred-and-sixty degrees. The Rossleague tower still retains its original cast-iron pivot. In the event of an attack the gun was worked by two of the garrison, the others remaining under cover and supplying those loading and firing the gun with ammunition, but ready to assume roof-top positions when required to fire on enemy landing parties.

Each individual tower was capable of withstanding a long siege, and in addition to about half a ton of gunpowder, would have been supplied with 100 round shot, 20 case and grape

70 Aerial view of Fort Camden, near Crosshaven, Co. Cork.

shot and up to 280 varied types of shell. Roundshot fired from a 24-pounder could make a respectable hole in a ship quite some way off-shore, whilst landing parties faced a barrage of case and grapeshot, and possibly a taste of Major Henry Shrapnel's recent invention, an exploding shell which burst in the air, showering infantry with splinters. In the event the Cork harbour Martellos saw no action during the Napoleonic Wars, although the Monning

Martello has the distinction of being the only Irish example to have ever been attacked. In December 1867 an Irish American Fenian, Francis Lomasney, alias Captain Mackey, surprised its garrison (albeit in a gentlemanly fashion) and made off with the contents of the magazine.

THE POST NAPOLEONIC PERIOD

Invasion scares did not end with Napoleon's downfall, and during the second half of the 19th century the British military establishment panicked on a number of occasions over the unpreparedness (both real and imagined) of Britain's coastal defences. In 1859 a Royal Commission was established to report on the state of the defences of the United Kingdom, the conclusions of which appeared in February 1860. In the opinion of the Commission Cork harbour possessed "great capabilities as a naval port", which in wartime would be of great strategic importance to the defence of both Ireland and the western approaches to England. Amongst its recommendations was that Forts Camden and Carlisle should be equipped with proper landward defences which would prevent their being taken in reverse, whilst their sea defences should be extended. As a direct result of the Royal Commission's report a truly staggering programme of fortress building and re-development was undertaken throughout Britain and Ireland, with no less than seventy-six forts and batteries being either completed or under construction by 1867.

The Commission's findings in regard to the defences of Cork harbour were quickly acted upon. The grand design of Britain's remodelled coastal defences was heavily influenced by the then Deputy Director of Works for fortifications, Lieutenant-Colonel Jervois, but responsibilty for the detailed design work on the Cork harbour fortifications was entrusted to Lieutenant-Colonel Fisher. The design of the new Fort Carlisle had been completed in 1860 but the extensive works undertaken on it were not completed until 1880. However, both the main ditch and parapet were completed between 1861 and 1863, although the work on the lower batteries, begun in 1864, was not completed until 1880. By 1875 thirty new guns had been added to the landward side of Fort Camden, which complemented the existing sea battery of twelve guns. The disposition of the harbour-facing batteries at Camden, however, was such that when guns with greater ranges were introduced the fort was not able to engage long-range targets on the open sea. Forts Westmorland, on Spike Island, Carlisle and Templebreedy (near Myrtleville) were now allotted this task and Camden was to provide cover for the lower harbour.

Nonetheless, Fort Camden did have some remarkable features which included a Brennan Torpedo system and a "disappearing coast gun". The torpedo system was developed by a Mayo-born inventor called Louis Philip Brennan. A series of cables operated from the shore enabled the torpedo's propellors and special steering vanes to be controlled, enabling shore-based operators to guide the torpedo on to its target. The Brennan Torpedo is the precursor of modern wire-guided missiles and has been hailed as the world's first guided missile. The disappearing coast gun differed radically from the casemated guns (i.e. guns emplaced in bomb-proof, vaulted chambers) installed at Fort Carlisle in the 1880s, in that the entire gun could be lifted above the parapet and lowered again for re-loading under cover.

Under the conditions laid down under the Treaty of 1921, the British retained the right to maintain naval facilities in Cork harbour and at other so-called "Treaty Ports", up until the late 1930s, when its military establishment decided that it was no longer in Britain's interest to maintain them. With the advent of World War II this decision was deeply regretted, but the receipt of assurances from the Irish Free State government of the time, that these ports would not be used against Britain in the event of war, also helped to influence the British decision to hand these facilties over to the Irish government. Under an agreement of April 1938 the Cork harbour forts, along with British installations in Ireland, were to be handed over to the Irish army; and in July of 1938 the Irish flag flew over Forts Camden, Carlisle, Westmorland and Templebreedy.

FIVE

Industrial Archaeology

Industrial archaeology has quite a distinguished pedigree in Ireland, even though the term itself was only coined as recently as 1955. The first industrial archaeological survey of any region in either Britain or Ireland focussed attention on the Lagan Valley around Belfast. Indeed, the first comprehensive industrial archaeological surveys conducted within the twenty-six counties have been undertaken by the Office of Public Works in County Cork, whilst the first detailed industrial archaeological survey of a southern Irish city has featured the city of Cork. The aims of industrial archaeology are exactly the same as of those of any other branch of archaeology, except that the period that it deals with focusses attention on the development of the landscape since the industrial revolution.

There are four main areas of study within industrial archaeology: (a) primary or extractive industries (e.g. mining and quarrying); (b) secondary or manufacturing industry (i.e. textiles and engineering); (c) transport and communications (e.g. roads and railways), and (d) Public Utilities (e.g. water supply, electricity). The main types of industrial activity conducted within the harbour area from around 1750 will be dealt with below under these headings

At the end of the 18th century Cork was the second city of Ireland, while its port and harbour were amongst the most strategically important within the British empire. Cork harbour had become the British navy's most important base in Ireland. British ships assembled under convoy at ports such as Portsmouth and proceeded to Cork - the most important transatlantic shipping port - to take on their provisions before continuing on to destinations in the Americas and the West Indies. The benefits accruing to Cork from this trade and the substantial British naval presence were considerable. By the end of the 18th century the harbour area had the largest butter market and sailcloth factory in Europe, and the largest units of gunpowder manufacture, distilling and brewing in Ireland. During the 19th century these industries experienced a gradual decline, but unlike other Irish regions the development of new industries did not adversely affect the fabric of the earlier industries. As a result many important industrial archaeological sites within the Cork harbour area have survived virtually intact.

EXTRACTIVE INDUSTRIES

QUARRYING

Substantial deposits of both carboniferous limestone and red sandstone have always been readily available within the Cork harbour area, a circumstance which is reflected in the architecture of the city of Cork and its environs. As we have already seen local limestone and sandstone were used to build the medieval town walls of Cork, and these stones continued to be used to great effect either individually or together in many of the city's 18th-and 19th-century buildings. Within the environs of the city limestone quarrying was confined to the area to the south of the River Lee, the most important quarries being the Carrigmore or Beaumont quarry and the Diamond quarry on the Mahon peninsula, and the Windmill Road (formerly Quarry Road) and Gillabbey quarries to the west of these. Carrigmore stone was used in many of the city's more imposing public buildings such as St. Finbarr's Cathedral, the Court House (1835) and the Cork Savings Bank (1842).

Limestone was also extensively quarried on Little Island and at Rostellan, the stone from which was used by Cork Harbour Commissioners to construct many of the the city's quaysides in the first half of the 19th century. Carrigacrump quarries near Cloyne had limestone which could be raised in large blocks, of a type favoured for the beds of steam engines. The foundation for the original steam engine of Wallis and Pollock's flax-spinning mill at Donnybrook, for example, was made with Carrigacrump stone. Quarries on Little Island and near Midleton also produced Cork "red marble" which was used for decorative purposes.

Throughout the last century many large kilns for burning limestone were at work within the harbour area, the end product of which was used as a bonding agent in construction, as a fertiliser, in the tanning process and for purifying gas. Most quarries would have had at least one lime kiln, but in the city's salt and lime works batteries of up to three kilns would have been at work. The expense of importing coal simply for burning lime could not, in many cases, be justified by many lime burners. And so in Cork and in other Irish ports lime burners hit on the expedient of using the heat from the lime kiln for purifying imported English rock salt in metal pans. Dairy salt was, of course, an extremely important commodity, being used by farmers throughout Munster in the manufacture of butter.

Sandstone was quarried principally within the environs of the city, at Richmond Hill, the Backwatercourse, Sunday's Well Road and at what was the most important sandstone quarry within the Cork harbour area, "Flaherty's" or the Brickfield Quarry on the Lower Glanmire Road. Local red sandstone was used in many important buildings such as St Vincent's Church in Sunday's Well and the Corporation Waterworks, but by and large stonemason's found the local limestone much easier to work with.

In the second half of the 18th century up to three million bricks per year were manufactured in the area now occupied by Kent railway station. However, the smoke from the clamps in which the bricks were fired caused a public nuisance, which an act of Parliament effectively removed in 1778. Thereafter it became illegal to make bricks within a two-mile radius of the city, and the mayor was empowered to destroy any clamps which did. However, by the early decades of the 19th century brickmaking had commenced on the slobs of the Douglas estuary. There were three brickfields here by 1842, providing about three months work every year for up to fifty-six people. The brick itself was generally of poor quality and was generally only used for internal walls or for external walls which would be plastered over. Transportation by water for such a bulky commodity was essential, and it was generally necessary for brickmakers to own their own boats. James Joyce, for example, a salt and lime manufacturer of South Terrace, Ballinlough quarry owner and Douglas brickmaker, owned no less than two skiffs, four large mud boats, two lighters and a hooker when he became bankrupt in 1852.

The absence of a local brickmaking industry within the harbour area for the greater part of

71. Eighteenth-century miller's house at Lee Mills, Cork, showing use of red sandstone and limestone building stone type-ical of many 18th-and 19th-century industrial buildings in Cork City.

the 18th century had led to the importation of Dutch brick, which generally entered the port as ballast. Examples of this brick (which is markedly much thinner than either English or home-produced bricks), can still be seen on the South Mall. Nonetheless, up until the mid-19th century even the bricks manufactured at Youghal could not really equal the quality of imported English "Bridgewater" bricks. But, from 1858 up until around 1914, a quality facing brick was produced at the Belvelly brickworks on Great Island. Belvelly brick was used in the extension to the Cork School of Design (now part of the Crawford Art Gallery) and in the Union Quay Constabularly Barracks. However, both Youghal and Belvelly brick had a solid competitor in Ballinhassig brick, which was first used to effect within the city in the Model School on Anglesea Street, completed in 1864.

Around the mid-19th century silica clay was discovered, but not immediately exploited, in the Rostellan area. Indeed, it was not until the early 1900s that the Department of Agricultural and Technical Education for Ireland began to draw attention to these deposits by arranging for a Cork contractor to dig some of it out. This was shipped to England and in 1902 a set of fine China made from Rostellan silica clay was commissioned and displayed. Despite the obvious success of this experiment these deposits did not begin to be commercially exploited until the 1920s. Some of the clay was shipped to England, although the foundry of Ford's tractor works at City Park provided a ready local market. The Rostellan mine was short-lived, closing in 1928, but the Cloyne deposits were worked up until the early 1960s and were shipped from Ballynacorra to other Irish ports and British potteries.

MANUFACTURING INDUSTRIES

BREWING

In 1785 no less a connoisseur of English and Irish porter than William Dyott reported that he found Cork porter "the very worse". Indeed, the level of production at Beamish and Crawford's 'Cork Porter Brewery", established in 1792, was only exceeded by Guinness' brewery in 1833. Parts of Beamish and Crawford's brewery (principally those on the west side of the present complex of buildings) date to the late 18th century. Despite the recent addition of modern fermentation vessels and a new bottling plant, which has dramatically altered the configuration of the complex, a number of important items of 19th-century plant have survived in situ. Of these the most striking is the electrically-driven malt-milling plant, all of which was still in complete working order in the late 1970s. In 1992 Beamish and Crawford celebrated its bi-centenary and is clearly Cork's most enduring large-scale industrial enterprise.

The main buildings of the Lee Porter Brewery on Prospect Row, built between 1796-97, survive largely intact. This brewery passed into the hands of Charles Henry Leslie (a co-founder of the Gunpowdermills at Ballincollig in 1794) in 1799, and later came under the control of Beamish and Crawford. Leslie had for a short period been one of Beamish and Crawford's main local competitors, and after its takeover by them in the early 19th century, it was converted for use as a maltings (see below). The maltings of other Cork breweries established in the 18th century, Drinan's of Cove Street and Copperthwaite's on Wandesford's Quay, have also survived. The buildings of large 18th/19th-century breweries such as Lane's South Gate Brewery (now a car park and petrol station) and St Fin-barr's Brewery (on a site now occupied

72. Late nineteenth-century malt-milling plant in Beamish and Crawford's brewery.

73. The Lee Porter Brewery, Prospect Row, Cork, built between 1796-97. This brewery was bought by Beamish and Crawford in 1813 and was later incorporated into their maltings.

by the School of Art on Sharman Crawford Street) have been less fortunate. The "Lady's Well Brewery", which became the second largest brewing enterprise in Cork, was established by the Murphy family in 1856. The facade of the Foundling Hospital, in and around which the brewery was built, can still be seen on Leitrim Street, though in recent years a large number of the original buildings have been demolished to enable the installation of new plant. The enormous malthouse complex, at the southern end of the surviving complex, has recently been adapted for modern use.

DISTILLING

At a relatively early period the distilling industry in Cork was of both local and national importance. As early as 1802 a 1,179-gallon still was in operation at Walker and Brown's distillery at Crosses Green, which at that time was the largest in Ireland. The greater part of the 19th century, indeed, was generally favourable to the development of Cork's many distilleries, which were amongst the first industries within the harbour area to embrace the new technology of steam power. Three of the city's main distilleries had installed steam engines manufactured by the famous English firm of Boulton & Watt, of the Soho Foundry, Birmingham: Walker's of Crosses Green (in c.1800), Wise's of the North Mall (1808), and Hewitt's of Watercourse Road (1811-12). They were amongst the first in the country to do so.

For the most part the distilleries established within the harbour area produced pot still whiskey, but by the early 1830s two city distilleries – the Watercourse Distillery and the

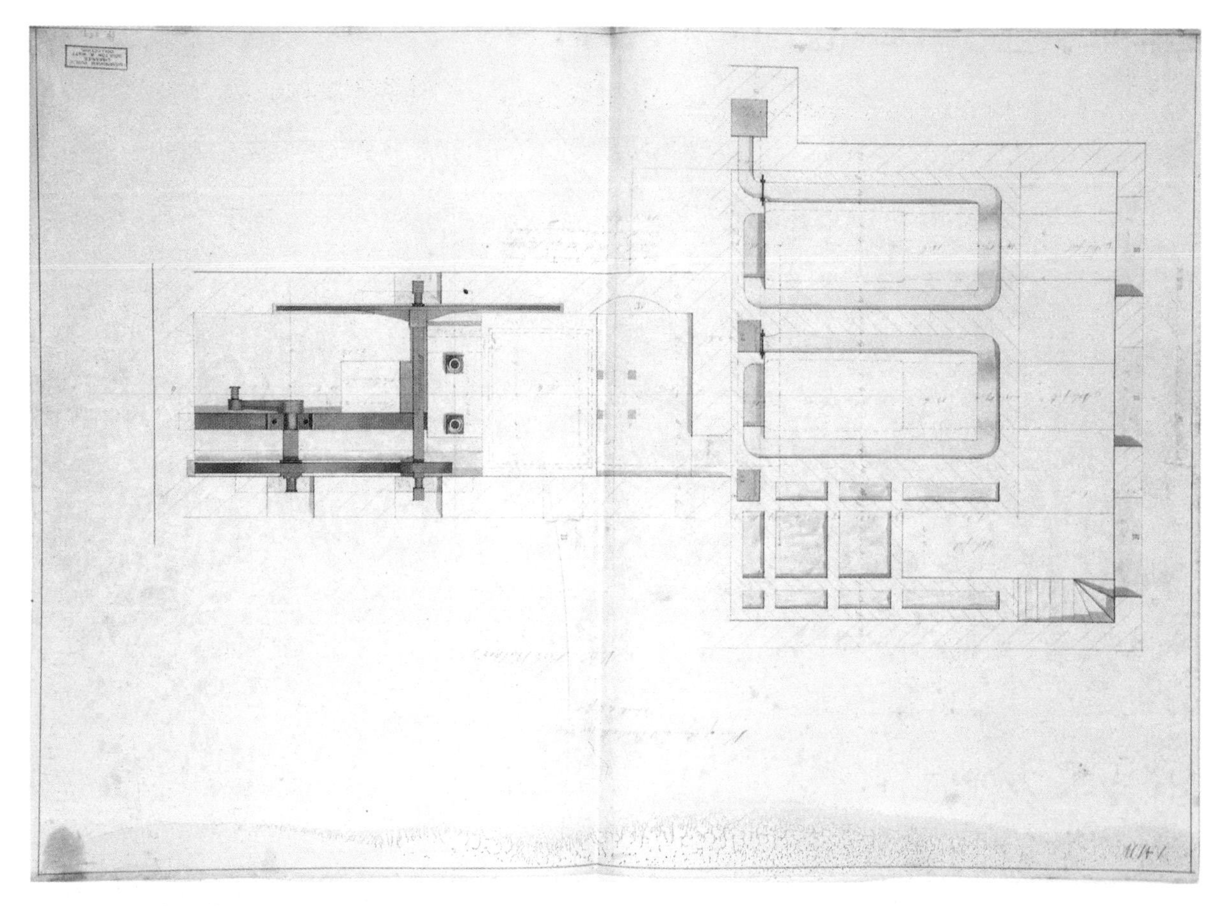

74. Drawing of Boulton and Watt steam engine, dated 1805, installed in Walker's Distillery at Crosses Green, Cork. This engine was the first of its type to be used in an Irish distillery.

Millfield Distillery – were operating what were called patent or continuous stills. Pot still distillation involved a series of repeated distillations and large amounts of coal as fuel, an expensive commodity which had to be imported. The use of patent stills, on the other hand, enabled distillation to become a continuous process with a consequent saving in fuel. The patent still installed in the Watercourse Distillery in 1833 was of the type patented in 1830 by a former Inspector General of Excise in Ireland, Aeneas Coffey. However, the patent still employed in the Millfield Distillery (established in 1783 on a site now occupied by the Millfield flax-spinning and weaving mill) sometime before 1836, was of the St. Marc type, and is the earliest recorded use of this type of patent still in Ireland.

The North Mall Distillery was established in 1779, and for most of its operational lifetime was associated with the brothers William and Thomas Wise. Very little of the complex, which covered upwards of twenty three acres in 1887, has survived. Most of the buildings nestling under the sandstone escarpment beneath Sunday's Well Road have been demolished, and very few of the original buildings have survived. The main granaries, which are built of locally quarried sandstone, have loading doors facing Sunday's Well Road. Part of a late medieval ogee-head window has been incorporated into the western corner of this building, and was popularly believed to have come from the adjacent Franciscan Abbey, long since

75. Eighteenth-century granaries at the Watercourse Distillery, Cork.

76. Midleton Distillery, Co. Cork, with tail race of distillery in foreground.

77. Malting kiln at Midleton Distillery.

demolished. However, as this window has initials carved upon it, there is little likelihood that it was ever used in a monastery. In 1877-78 the Cork Distilleries Company built an enormous 160ft chimney stack up against the rockface to Sunday's Well Road, the discharge from which was designed to replace five earlier chimneys. The brick base of this stack, complete with an inscription plaque, may be seen near the eastern end of Sunday's Well Road. The 230ft-long mill weir ("Wise's Weir") and the western section of the millrace served by it also survive upstream from the Lee Maltings. The production of the distillery's main brand, "Wise's Old Pot Still Whiskey", ceased in the 1920s after a large section of the complex was destroyed by fire, though the site has continued in use as bonded stores by Irish Distillers.

In stark contrast to the mixed fortunes of the North Mall complex the buildings of the massive Watercourse Distillery, founded in 1792, have survived largely intact. In 1828 it was the second largest distillery in the city, after Wise's, and was the only distillery within the city to have a Coffey patent still installed. The foundations of the distillery were quarried out of the sandstone bedrock, and most of the stone removed in this fashion appears to have been incoporated into the 18th-century granaries and still house which command the higher ground on the site. Until its incorporation into the Cork Distilleries Company in 1868 the Watercourse Distillery was controlled by the Hewitt family. A rationalisation plan introduced by the C.D.C.in the 1880s, however, concentrated whiskey production at the North Mall plant and in 1916 new plant was installed by the Cork Yeast Company to manufacture bakers' yeasts.

Immediately north of the Watercourse Distillery are the remains of the Green Distillery, which for most of the present century functioned as bonded warehouses. It was established by Robert Allan and Denis Corcoran in 1783 and was one of the city's smaller distilleries. By 1812 it was under the control of the brothers Joseph and Thomas Shee. Joseph Shee was clearly the greatest innovator amongst Cork distillers, as he actually patented his own continuous still, one of which was at work at the Green Distillery on Thomas Davis Street in 1850. However, when George Waters & Co. took over the distillery in 1851, Shee's own patent still was replaced with traditional pot stills. Cork Corporation demolished the greater part of this distillery in 1988.

In 1825 James Murphy established what was to become the largest distillery in the harbour area within the buildings of Lynch's woollen mill at Midleton (see below). Midleton Distillery, along with the Bushmills Distillery near Portrush in Co. Antrim, is now only one of two working distilleries in Ireland. It is also clearly the best preserved, the original distillery being left virtually unscathed when it was replaced by an entirely modern one built in 1975. Not only have the original maltings and grain stores been preserved but what are surely the most remarkable survivals of 19th-century distilling plant in Ireland, which included the world's largest pot still, survive *in situ*. The distillery's two steam engines also survive, one of which is in its original position, the other now on display in the Irish Museum of Steam at Straffan in Co. Kildare. An enormous cast-iron waterwheel, which dates to 1852, and which is still in perfect working order, also survives on

78. Cast-iron suspension waterwheel at Midleton Distillery, built by William Fairbairn of Manchester in 1852.

79. Furlong's Lapp's Quay Flour Mill, Cork city.

the north side of the original woollen mill building. The Midleton Distillery is the most important industrial archaeological site of its type in Ireland.

FLOUR MILLING.

From the medieval period up until the late 19th century running water was the main power source for the vast majority of flour mills built within the harbour area. Water-powered wheels turned anything from two to fifteen pairs of millstones, in mills situated within or immediately adjacent to towns and villages within the harbour. From around the 1830s onwards steam engines were installed in the larger mills to enable them to operate continuously during the summer months. Even in Ireland the volume of water in rivers and streams tended to be severely curtailed during the summer, a period during which many mills could only be worked for about six hours per day. In the 1850s water turbines began to be used within the greater Cork area in sawmills, linseed oil mills and in flour mills. In many instances these eventually replaced more traditional waterwheels. For the most part, however, mills which used traditional grinding stones tended to employ steam engines only as a back-up.

The main surviving water-powered mills of note within the harbour area are within the city. St Dominick's Mill, near St Mary's of the Isle Convent, may well have been built on an earlier medieval site. Most of the surviving buildings are 18th-century. Like most of the water-powered mills established within the city it suffered from a phenomenon called tidal backwatering, where the incoming tide flooded its outlet channel and prevented the waterwheel from turning. In the first half of the 19th century its water power (taken from the south channel of the Lee) allowed it to operate with two sets of millstones for up to six months in the year. But the raising of the Corporation Waterworks' weir in the late 1850s effectively ended its usefulness as a water-powered mill, but by this period the installation of a steam engine enabled it to operate on a 24-hour basis, regardless of the incoming tide.

The Crosses Green Mill (latterly part of Harte's Sawmills) appears to be an 18th-century foundation. Its internal machinery was remodelled by the famous Scottish engineer, John Rennie, in 1820, whose son designed the new docks at Rushbrooke for the Cork shipbuilder, Joseph Wheeler (see below). In 1836 its 45 hp waterwheel was the largest at work in the city, but by the 1840s flour production at the mills appears to have been entirely given over to steam power.

In 1787 the Cork glassmaker and brewer, Atwell Hayes, established what were to become known as the Lee Mills or "Hayes' Mills" on the north channel of the Lee. The mills, which operated with three wooden waterwheels, and its bakehouses were leased to Beamish and Crawford (who had purchased the adjoining Lee Brewery in 1813) between 1813-20. Between 1825 and 1831 the existing six and seven-storey buildings on the quayside were built on the site of the original Hayes' Mills by Beamish and Crawford. The three large iron waterwheels were made by Steele's Vulcan foundry on Lancaster Quay and the original machinery which powered these by the English firm of Peele, Williams and Peele of Manchester, who also made a steam engine for Midleton distillery. In their heyday the mills operated 15 sets of millstones, which made them the largest at work within the harbour area. They were also the last water-powered flour mills to operate within the city. Shortly after 1881 the mills were converted for use as malting floors by Beamish and Crawford and were quickly incorporated into their adjacent Nile Street or Lee Maltings.

TEXTILES

A number of the present day suburbs of the city have evolved out of settlements associated with textile manufactories dating to the 18th century. The creation of Douglas village, for example, is

80.The Lee Mills, Cork, established in 1797 and rebuilt by Beamish and Crawford in the period 1825-31 . The mills were incorporated into Beamish and Crawford's adjacent malting operation in the early 1880s.

81.Flax-spinning mill at Donnybrook, Co. Cork, built in 1866 by Cork architect Richard Bolt Brash for Wallis and Pollock. the design of the building was based on contemporary Belfast mills.

traditionally associated with the settlement of Ulster weavers there in the early decades of the 18th century and the subsequent success of the sailcloth factory. In 1745 some 250 operatives were employed at Donnybrook near Douglas village, along with 500 spinners outside it. A number of Huguenot families were instrumental in ensuring its success though it is the Besnard family who were outright owners from the early 1780s, and who were the first in Ireland to adopt water-powered flax-spinning machinery, who are normally associated with the factory. The importance of this enterprise in employment terms alone is exemplified by the fact that, in 1810, 1,000 hands were employed. Mixed fortunes followed in the wake of the Napoleonic Wars and by 1820 all flax spinning at the Douglas factory ceased. The surviving multi-storey flax-spinning mill at Donnybrook was designed and built by the Cork architect

82.Cork Flax-Spinning and Weaving Company's mill at Millfield on the northern outskirts of Cork city, built on the site of a former distillery between 1864-66. The mill was designed by the Belfast architects, Boyd and Platt.

83. O'Brien Brothers wool-spinning and weaving mill at Douglas, Co. Cork, built in 1882.

and antiquarian, Richard Bolt Brash, for Hugh and James Wheeler Pollock in 1866. Its essential design, like that of the Millfield flax-spinning mill (see above), was modelled closely on contemporary Belfast mills, and indeed neither mill would be out of place on the Crumlin Road.

The flax-spinning mill built by the Cork Flax Spinning and Weaving Company between 1864 and 1866, on the site of a former distillery at Millfield, is the best surviving example of its type in the Irish Republic. It was designed by the Belfast architects, Boyd and Platt, and was equipped with the most up-to-date steam engines then available. The mill was managed using northern Irish and Dutch expertise. Unfortunately, the early company did not have the resources to survive the depression which followed in the wake of the American Civil War and the mill was put up for auction in 1871. Shortly afterwards it re-opened only to be closed again in 1885, being re-opened once again in 1889, but on this occasion on a more sounder footing. At the turn of the century it was also operating looms for weaving, and, by 1919, was employing upwards on 1,000 people. For late 19th-century visitors arriving in Cork by train the Millfield mill must have appeared as a potent symbol of local enterprise. It was, indeed, a local attempt to emulate the success of the Ulster linen industry.

In the 18th century Cork county was the very heart of the Irish woollen industry. A number of large factories enagaged in woollen manufacture were established within the greater Cork area, one of the largest and most short-lived of which was Lynch's mill at Midleton. In the late 1790s Lynch spent the then enormous sum of £20,000 on the construction of a multi-storey wool-spinning mill. It was powered by two waterwheels and the watercourse supplying it was about two miles long. It could not, however, survive the depression of the early 1800s when it was forced to close, but was later to become incorporated into Murphy's Distillery. Wallis and Pollock's flax-spinning mill at Donnybrook became the nucleus for Morrough Brothers woollen and worsted cloth factory, which was fitted out in 1890. In 1882 O'Brien Brothers built a new woollen spinning and weaving mill at Douglas village, most of which still survives. The mill buildings, which are built throughout with local limestone, are most unusual in that, by this period, brick would have been the obvious and perhaps most economical choice.

SHIPBUILDING

In 1776 some 40% of the Irish ships on Lloyd's register were built at Cork and, throughout the 19th and early 20th centuries, shipbuilding in the general harbour area was to remain an important industry. The first steamship built in Ireland, the *City of Cork,* was built at Hennessy's of Passage West in 1815, whilst in 1816 the *Waterloo,* which was built at the same yard, was equipped with the first marine steam engines built in Ireland. The engines were built at Cork's Hive Iron Foundry, and so the *Waterloo* earned the distinction of becoming the first wholly Irish-built steamship. In the early decades of the 19th century the shipbuilding yards on the Lower Glanmire Road were the most important in the country, as local shipbuilders took full advantage of the opportunities that the growth of the port offered to them. By the late 1840s no less than four shipyards were at work in the city and, in 1844, the local firm of Lecky and Beale launched the first iron ship to be built at Cork. The last ship to be built at the Lower Glanmire Road was launched at George Robinson's yard in 1872. One of the original slipways of the Cork shipyards can still be seen in the present Harbour Commissioners yards on the Lower Glanmire Road.

In 1835 the first large shipyard at Passage was completed and was later to be renamed the "Victoria" in 1840. A second dry dock, the "Albert", was completed in 1855. In the 1850s the shipyard designed by Sir John Rennie for

84.Perrott's Hive Iron Foundry, Cork, established in 1810.

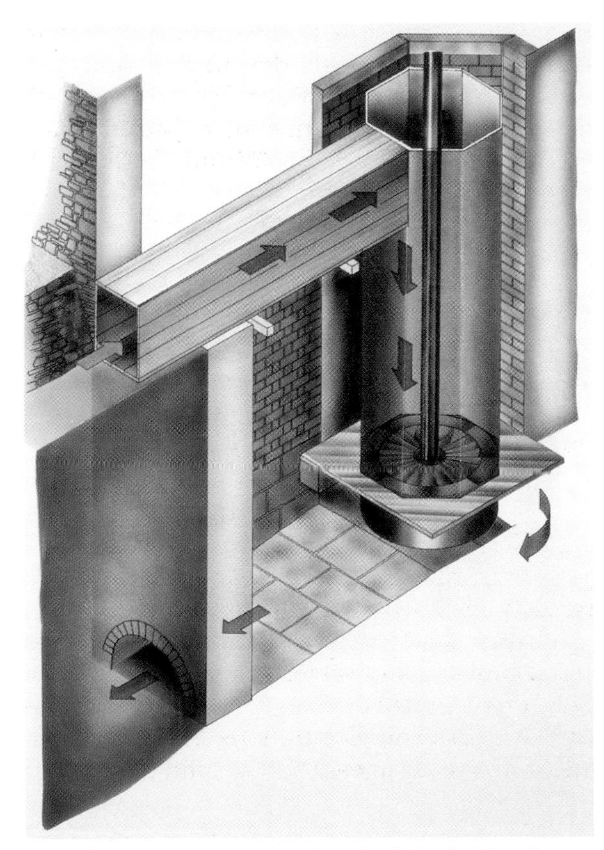

85.Reconstruction of water turbine built by the Hive Iron foundry, in 1855, for powering sawmill machinery at the Royal Gunpowdermills, Ballincollig, Co. Cork. This is the earliest-known example of its type to have been used in Ireland.

Joseph Wheeler at Rushbrooke was completed and was amalgamated with the Passage yard in 1870.

IRON WORKING

The city of Cork in the 19th century was an important centre of the Irish heavy engineering industry, but only at the Hive Iron Works on Hanover Street, established in 1810, have any buildings directly associated with this activity survived. The works were set up by two English millwrights, Barnes and Atkinson, who supplied flax spinning machinery for the Douglas mills in the early 1800s. For the greater part of the 19th century, however, the Hive Iron Works was closely associated with the Perrott family. Its products, which include everthing from the 19th-century bollards on the city's quaysides to a rare form of water turbine installed in Ballincollig gunpowder mills, can still be found all over the greater Cork region. The first marine steam engines built in Ireland, as was seen above, were also built there. Part of the original foundry complex can still be seen on Hanover Street next door to the recently completed social security office, whilst Perrott's retail warehouse, built in 1829, still stands at the western end of Washington Street.

TRANSPORT AND COMMUNICATIONS

THE PORT OF CORK

The main factor affecting the physical development of the port of Cork for the greater part of the 19th century was the inability of vessels of larger draught to discharge their cargoes afloat at the city quaysides. Indeed, as late as 1846, the city quays themselves only extended from St. Patrick's Bridge on the north channel and Parliament Bridge on the south channel, to an area about 200 yards east of the Custom House. There were no buoys or lighthouses to mark the main channel and large vessels could only reach the city quays on the spring tides, where all vessels had to lie aground. For the greater part of the 19th century, therefore, cargoes were transhipped to "lighters" at Passage West, an arrangement which was often included in shipping contracts. Regardless of such arrangements, masters of vessels were nearly always reluctant to venture as far as the city quays.

The first steps by the Harbour Commissioners to improve the city's docks were initiated in the 1850s, when the "Lee" dredger was commissioned, and the debris from its early operations was transported ashore to form the Marina embankment. These first practical steps were further supplemented by the lighting and buoying of the main channel from Horse Head to Cork which began in 1850.

In 1874 an important construction project which would enable overseas shipping to dock safely at Cork was begun, involving the con-

86. Cork, Blackrock and Passage Railway terminus at Albert Street, Cork, built in 1873 to replace the original terminus at City Park. Closed in 1932.

struction of timber jetties along Victoria Quay and the dredging of the areas adjacent to these to a depth of 20ft at low water. The project was completed by 1875, with the end result being the provision of an extra 1,000ft of deep water berthage, later extended to form the Victoria Wharf. A further dredger was commissioned in 1876 to undertake the important task of improving the main channel by dredging a 250ft-wide section of it to a depth of 14ft from Horse Head to Cork, a task which was not completed until 1884. The main phase of the development of the city's quaysides ended in 1903, when the existing wooden wharfs were extended up the north channel to Warren's Place, and on the south channel as far as Albert Street railway station.

RAILWAYS

In the 19th century no less than six railway companies were operating in the harbour area.

THE CORK BLACKROCK AND PASSAGE RAILWAY

The first six-and-a-half miles of standard gauge line (i.e 5ft 3in) from the Cork terminus at City Park on Victoria Road to Passage were opened in 1850. Cork Corporation's desire to develop the adjacent quayside, however, forced the railway company to close the City Park station and relocate at Albert Street (a short distance from the former) in 1873. After the opening of the Queenstown extension of the Cork-Youghal line in 1862 the company felt obliged to extend their line as far as Crosshaven. This was the second of Cork's narrow gauge lines, which was opened in 1904. All of the existing route was later to be changed to narrow gauge (i.e. 3ft). The C.B.& P.R., Cork city's earliest railway, was closed in 1932. Albert Street Station was converted for the use of the Cork Metal Co., though for the most part the station building is still recognizable as such.

THE GREAT SOUTHERN AND WESTERN RAILWAY

One of the main engineering problems facing William Dargan in relation to the construction of the Thurles-Cork section of the Great South Western Railway was the difficult terrain leading up to and lying on the outskirts of the city of Cork. Two impressive viaducts were built within five miles of the intended terminus on Penrose Quay, one to span the river valley occupied by the Monard Iron Works, the other to carry the line across the Kilnap Glen, an area also traversed by the Mallow road. Both of these viaducts are still in service carrying the main Cork-Dublin line.

The G.S.& W.R. reached the Blackpool area of the city in October 1849 but, owing to the immediate problem of extending the line to Penrose Quay, a temporary terminus was built at Kilbarry near Blackpool. Preparations for the railway tunnel to Penrose Quay began in 1847 when the four airshafts which traversed the high ground above the river were sunk. The tunnel, 1,355 yards long, which is currently the longest still in use in Ireland, took eight years to complete and was formally opened in 1855. Penrose Quay railway station was also opened in 1855 and remained in use until 1893 when the present Glanmire Road (Kent) Station was opened. The shell of the large, cut-limestone engine shed built in the 1850s still stands, as does the original station master's office of the Penrose Quay Station. The present station was built both to replace the smaller Penrose Quay terminus and the Cork terminus of the Youghal railway at Summerhill. Within its foyer an original Bury engine ("no.36"), which was made for the G.S.& W.R. by Bury, Curtis and Kennedy of Liverpool in 1847, is on open display. During its working life this engine had covered over 350,000 miles when it was withdrawn from service in 1875. The rails on which it stands are of the original 92lbs per yard, G.S.& W.R. type.

THE CORK BANDON AND SOUTH COAST RAILWAY.

The first section of the line from Bandon to Ballinhassig (some 13 or so miles from Cork)

87. Glanmire Road Station, Cork (latterly Kent Station), opened in 1893 to replace original Great Southern and Western Cork terminus on Penrose Quay.

88. Bury, Curtis & Kennedy engine built in 1847 for Great Southern and Western Railway Company, at Kent Station, Cork. The engine is displayed on original G.S. & W.R. rails.

opened in 1849, but the opening of the Cork-Ballinhassig section had to wait until 1851 and the completion of a 900-yard tunnel through Goggin's Hill and the construction of the impressive cast-iron viaduct at Chetwynd. The impressive cut-limestone terminus building on Albert Quay is the oldest surviving station building within the harbour area. The line was closed by C.I.E. in 1961 and the former railway cutting within the immediate environs of the city now carries the south city link road.

THE CORK, YOUGHAL AND QUEENSTOWN RAILWAY.

This was essentially a series of link lines which connected Youghal and Cobh with the G.S.& W.R. network via Cork. The first section of the line, between Midleton and Dunkettle, opened in 1859 and was finally extended to Youghal in 1860; the stretch from Dunkettle to Summerhill Station at Cork was opened later in the same year. A further extension to Queenstown was later built to deal with the transatlantic liner traffic and to handle the mails. The original three cast-iron foot bridges, built in 1860 to accommodate the inhabitants of Carrig House, Belle Vue Terrace and Woodhill Terrace, whose access to the Lower Glanmire Road was effectively cut off by the railway, have also survived. Summerhill Station was closed along with the Penrose Quay Station in 1893, when the traffic from both stations was directed to Glanmire Road. Up until quite recent times the line carried excursion traffic to Youghal, but in 1992 Iarnród Éireann have begun to lift sections of the line.

THE CORK AND MACROOM DIRECT RAILWAY.

From its opening in 1866, to 1879 when the company opened its own terminus at Capwell, the Cork-Macroom line shared the Albert Quay Station with the C.B.& S.C.R. However, the Cork and Macroom Co. eventually fell out with the C.B.& S.C.R. about the leasing arrangements (amongst other things) at Albert Quay, which prompted its decision to build a separate terminus for its trains at Capwell in 1879. After the railway amalgamation of 1925, however, the Macroom bound trains were once again run from Albert Quay. The fine brick station house at Capwell still survives, though most of the railway yards have long since been converted for use as a bus depot. The Macroom line was closed in 1953.

THE CORK AND MUSKERRY LIGHT RAILWAY.

Unlike the C.B.& P.R. which was originally built to the Irish standard gauge and later converted to narrow gauge, the Cork and Muskerry Light Railway *("The Muskerry Tram")* which was incorporated under the Tramways Act of 1883, was always intended to be a narrow gauge line. The first eight-and-three-quarter miles of line between Cork and Blarney Castle were opened in 1887, and between 1888 and 1893, this was extended to Coachford and Donoughmore. In 1898 the Cork City Tramways system opened which created a unique situation insofar as Britain and Ireland are concerned whereby electric and steam tramways ran side by side along a public road. From its terminus on the Bishop's Marsh, adjacent to Western Road, the line crossed the Lee and became a tramway for about four miles along the Western Road and the Carrigrohane straight, beyond which it broke off into open countryside like a normal railway. The C.& M.L.R. was one of the earliest casualties of motor transport in the Cork area, closing in 1934. The Western Road terminus along with the bridge over the Lee were demolished in the 1950s.

THE CORK CITY RAILWAYS AND WORKS CO.

In 1912 a rail link was opened between the Albert Quay and Glanmire Road stations, which enabled rolling stock to pass from the west Cork line onto the G.S.& W.R. Two iron lift bridges, Clontarf and Brian Boru, were specially constructed for this purpose. The Brian Boru and Clontarf bridges are still in use though not for rolling stock, this latter activity ending in the 1960s. Some sections of the track were still in position up until the late 1970s, though the only surviving rails which remain *in situ* are those on the Custom House Quay. The curved portion of the original line, which cut through from Brian Boru Street on to the Lower Glanmire Road, has now been resurfaced for use as a pedestrian thoroughfare.

TRAMWAYS

Between the years 1872-1875 a private company operated a horse tramway service in the centre of Cork. The tram lines were removed by the Corporation in 1876 and no physical remains of this enterprise have survived. Cork was amongst the first Irish towns to have a network of electric trams, a service which ran from 1898

89. Albert Quay terminus of Cork, Bandon & South Coast Railway, opened in 1851. This line was closed in 1961.

to 1931. The Cork Electric Tramways and Lighting Company operated three cross-city routes: (a) Blackpool-Douglas; (b) Summerhill-Sunday's Well; and (c) Tivoli-Blackrock. The tramway depot at Albert Road has survived virtually intact, and contains the only surviving examples of the original tram tracks at a gauge of 2ft.11in. The street track and its associated brick paving were laid by a company owned by William Martin Murphy, who was later to become a chairman of the Cork company. The fleet of 35 tram cars was built in England by the Brush Electrical and Engineering Co. at Loughborough. The tramway company also owned the Albert Road coal-fired electricity generating station from which, in addition to generating electricity to run its fleet of trams, it also supplied electricity to local consumers by arrangement with the Corporation.

BRIDGES ACROSS THE RIVER LEE

The single most important factor affecting the topography of the city of Cork has been the division of the Lee into two main channels. Yet despite the later expansion of the city beyond its medieval walls, as late as 1761 only two bridges - the North and South Gate bridges - actually spanned the main channels. The future expansion of the city thus relied on the provision of bridges that would communicate with new areas of settlement and relieve pressure of use on the existing bridges.

Part of the present South Gate Bridge is believed to date to 1713, the eastern side being widened at a later date, and as such is the oldest bridge within the city environs. Clarke's Bridge was built in 1766 to link Clarke's Marsh with the expanding area west of the original city wall. The construction of this bridge also helped to alleviate congestion at the South Gate, which at that time was the principal entry point for traffic from the south of the county. Bridge-building in the 19th century was generally in step with the expansion of the city and began with Parliament Bridge which was completed in 1806. In 1820 a substantial treble-arched bridge was built across the southern channel of the Lee to allow direct access to the city from the west of the county. Originally named George IV Bridge (and now called the O'Neill- Crowley Bridge) this bridge diminished the importance of South Gate Bridge as the main access point into the city from the west and south-west of the county, traffic from which now tended to be deflected through Victoria Cross. Gaol Cross bridge, built in 1835, allowed access from the former County Gaol across the southern channel of the Lee to the Western Road, and for many years was an important access point to Queen's College (U.C.C.). Two further masonry multi-span bridges were to be built across the north channel of the Lee in the 19th century, Wellington Bridge, completed in 1830, Anglesea and St. Patrick's Bridge which opened in 1861.

Wellington (latterly Thomas Davis) Bridge was designed by Richard Griffiths and St. Patrick's Bridge by Sir John Benson; both of the latter are the two most imposing bridges within the city environs. In 1878 the lattice girder bridge known as St. Vincent's was built to link the North Mall residential area with the south side of the city, one of the last bridges built to span the Lee in that century. O'Donovan's Bridge, which linked O'Donovan's Road to Western Road was opened in 1902 and, as has already been seen, the Brian Boru and Clontarf railway bridges were built in 1911 to carry the rail connection between the Albert Quay and Glanmire Road stations. Finally, the remarkable suspension bridge linking the Mardyke with the Sunday's Well area of the city, and presented to its citizens by James Daly, was opened in 1928.

PUBLIC UTILITIES

WATER SUPPLY

An Act of 1762 enabled Cork Corporation to set up the Cork Pipe Water Company and to establish the city's first waterworks. The site for the waterworks was chosen at a point beyond the tidal reaches of the river, to the west of the Duke of Devonshire's mills and weir. The weir itself was used to provide a head of water for the water-powered pumps which supplied a

90. Cork Corporation Waterworks, established in 1762. The existing buildings date from 1888 onwards.

storage reservoir (the "city basin") on the adjacent hillside, from which water was led to the city, by gravity, in wooden water mains. The foundation stone of the original waterworks, which bears the inscription "Cork Pipe Water Company Established 1768" has been incorporated into the present turbine house.

The 18th-century pumping machinery and the reservoirs on the adjacent hillside were ill-equipped to meet the demands of the rapidly expanding 19th-century city. Under the Cork Bridges, Waterworks and Improvements Act of 1856, the Corporation was enabled to take over the Pipe Water Company and to borrow funds for the updating of the Waterworks. The work was entrusted to Sir John Benson, who replaced two of the existing three waterwheels with two water turbines in 1859 and installed a Cornish steam engine manufactured by the Belfast firm of McAdam Brothers. Benson also constructed two new reservoirs in 1858 and 1860 which were still in use until quite recently. Cast-iron water mains, manufactured by a Glasgow foundry, began to be imported from 1857 onwards to replace the Pipe Water Company's original wooden pipes. The pumping capacity of the waterworks was continually expanded throughout the 19th century, beginning in 1863 with the installation of two 40 hp steam engines to supplement the 35 hp waterwheel, two water turbines (total 110 hp) and a 90 hp Cornish engine. An additional steam engine was installed in 1869.

In 1876 an infiltration gallery for filtering water was under construction, but this was not fully operational until 1884. Up until this time the water of the River Lee was distributed throughout the city untreated, and this gallery was able to meet the demands of the city as late as 1928. The present day pumphouse adjacent to the river was completed in 1888, and the five turbines in it (all of which were still working until 1992) were installed between 1888 and 1916. In 1902 the Corporation found that it had no option but to rapidly update the existing waterworks, which by this period required a capacity to pump up to two-and-half million gallons of water per day. Three new pumping engines, supplied by the Belfast firm of Combe and Barbour, were built in 1905 and installed in the new engine house at the works between 1905-07. These engines were intended as a back-up for the five water turbines, whose productivity was curtailed during the summer months when water levels in the river normally dropped. The Cork Corporation Waterworks is the most important industrial archaeological site of its type in Ireland.

GAS

In 1816 a James O'Brien of Tuckey Street used his own privately manufactured gas to light his premises. The use of gas for public lighting commenced as early as 1826 when the United General Gas Company opened its works at Albert Road. The premises as depicted on the first edition of the Ordnance Survey are quite small, with four moderately sized gasholders. Only the elaborate gatehouse and part of the original workshops have survived, and, for the most part, the other 19th-century buildings (many of which are now derelict) appear to post-date the takeover of the original company by the Cork Gas Consumers Company in 1859. Towns such as Midleton also had their own gas works as did larger industrial installations such as the Millfield flax mill and Morrogh's Woollen mill at Donnybrook.

91. Cork Electric Tramways and Lighting Company's generating station at Albert Road, Cork, built in 1898.

ELECTRICITY AND PUBLIC LIGHTING

From at least the early 1890s onwards the larger industrial installations within the city, such as Beamish and Crawford's and Murphy's breweries, had private electrical generators for powering electric lighting and certain items of plant. As has been seen above Cork's first public electricity generating station was built by the Cork Electric Tramways and Lighting Company on Albert Road in 1898. The original generating plant consisted of three Babcock and Wilcox boilers, along with three McIntosh and Seymour side-crank tandem compound condensing engines, each running at 135 r.p.m. These latter were coupled direct to two six-pole 200kW. compound wound generators. Early in the 20th century three Beliss and Morcom steam engines and two Allis and Chalmers horizontal compound engines were installed. In 1918 a 1500kw. geared Curtis Turbine and D.C. generator was added to meet the city's vastly increased demand for electricity. The building of the Albert Road generating station along with the tram depot still survives.

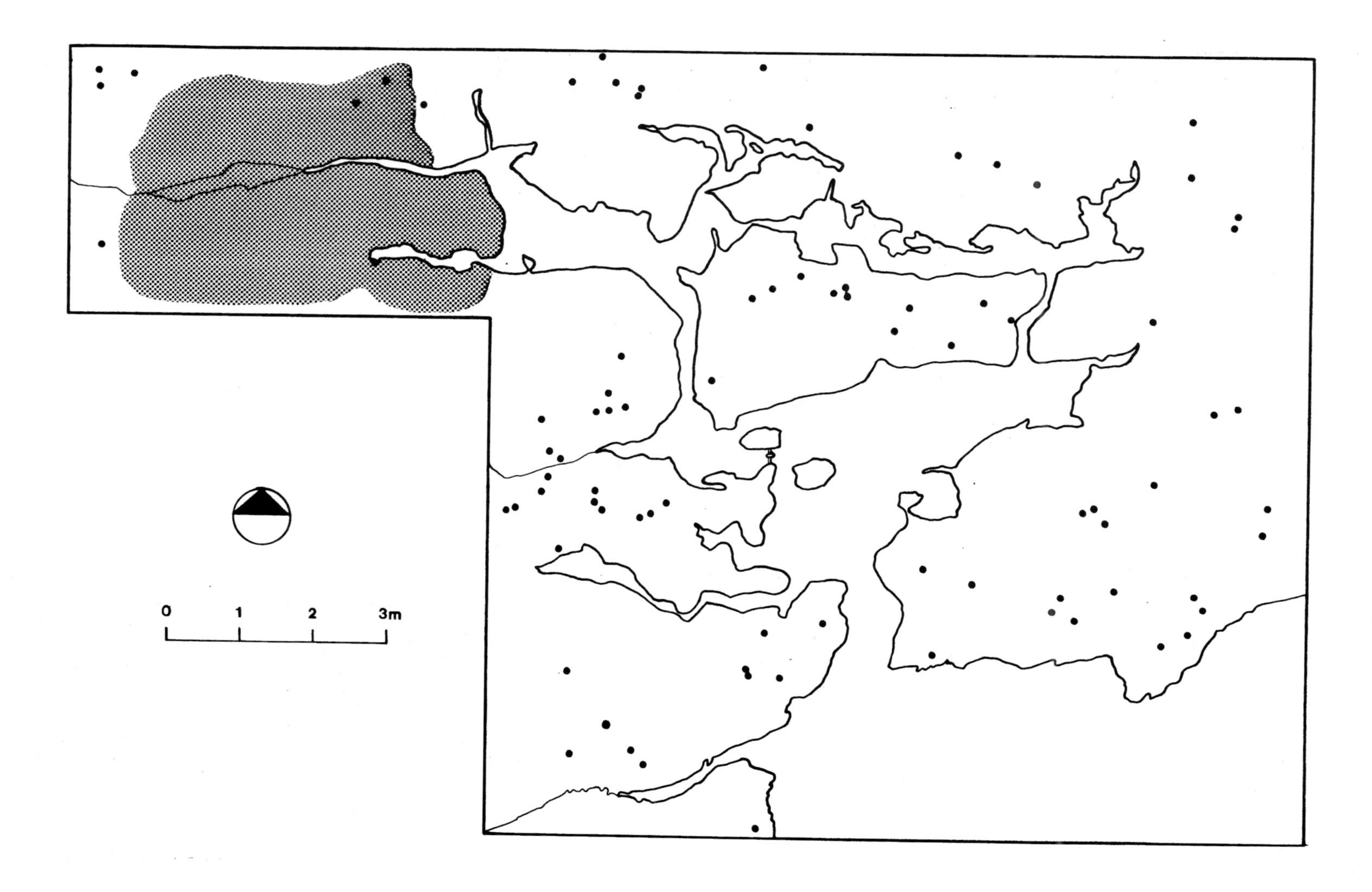

92. Distribution of ring forts in Cork harbour area.

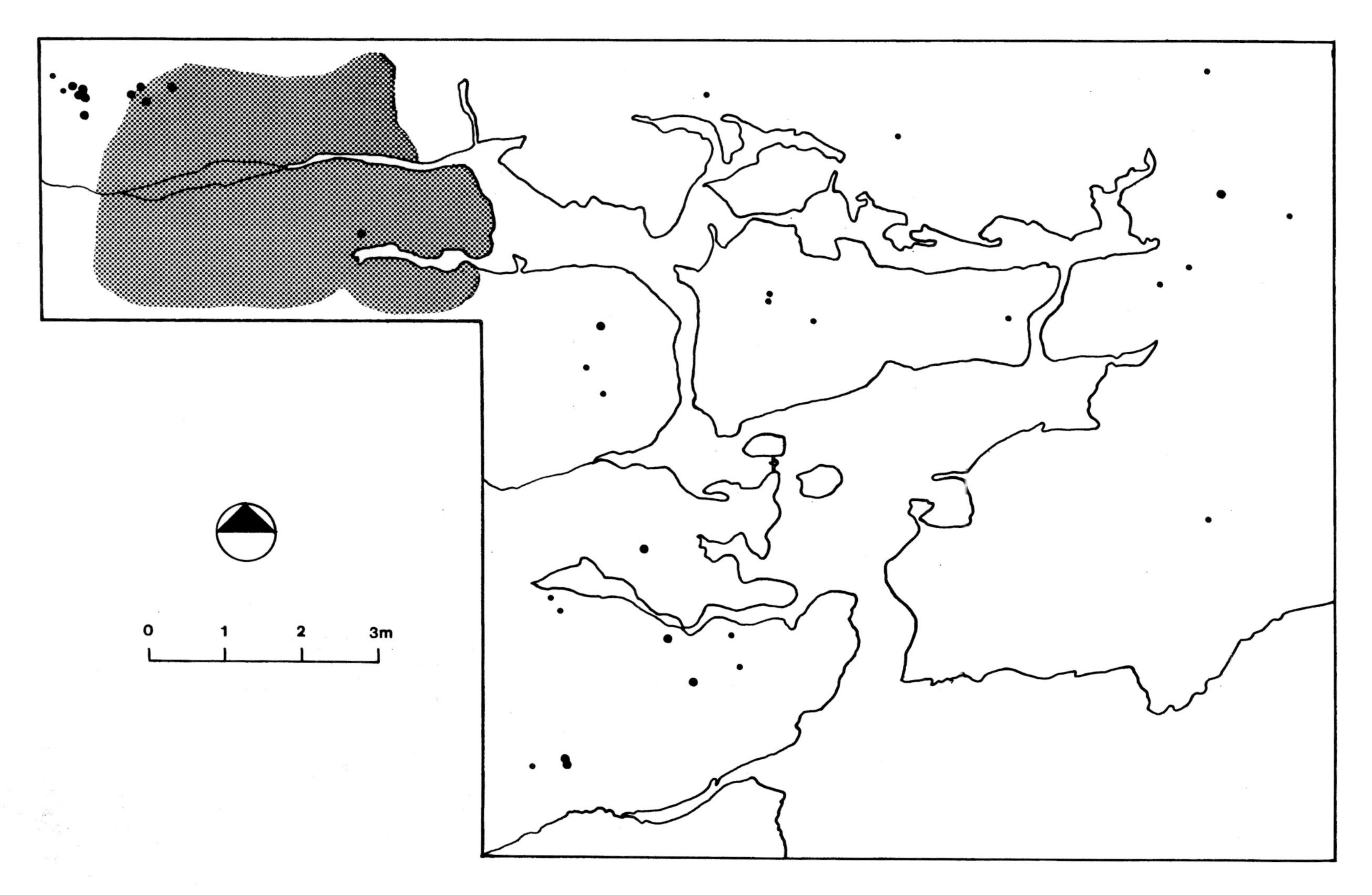

93. Distribution of standing stones and fulacht fiadha *in Cork harbour area.*

Further Reading

Abbreviations: J.C.H.A.S. (Journal of the Cork Historical and Archaeological Society); J.R.S.A.I. (Journal of the Royal Society of Antiquaries of Ireland).

CHAPTER ONE

Day, Robert "On a Hoard of Roman Coins found at Cuskinny", *J.C.H.A.S.,* IV, 1898, 49-51.

De Valera, Ruaidhri and O Nuallain, Sean *Survey of the Megalithic Tombs of Ireland, vol IV.* Dublin, 1982.

Gogan, L.S. "Irish Gold Lunulae: With Special Reference to a Pair from Midleton, Co. Cork", *J.C.H.A.S.,* XXXIV, 1934, 1-14.

Harbison, Peter *Pre-Christian Ireland. From the Earliest Settlers to the Early Celts.* London, 1988.

Mallory, J.P. and McNeill, T.F. *The Archaeology of Ulster from Colonization to Plantation.* Belfast, 1991. Chapters 1-5 of this book provide the most readable, short introduction to Irish prehistory currently available.

O'Kelly, M.J. "Some Prehistoric Monuments of Imokilly", *J.C.H.A.S.,* L, 1945, 10-23

"A Cinerary Urn from Oatencake, Midleton, Co. Cork", J.C.H.A.S., LII, 1947, 126-7.

"Excavations and Experiments in Irish Cooking Places", J.R.S.A.I., LXXXIV, 1954, 105-55.

"The Cork Horns, the Petrie Crown and the Bann Disc", J.C.H.A.S., LXVI, 1961, 1-12.

O'Kelly, Michael J. *Early Ireland. An Introduction to Irish Prehistory.* Cambridge, 1989.

O Riordain, Sean P. "A Prehistoric Burial at Ringabella, Co. Cork", *J.R.S.A.I.,* LXIV, 1934, 86-89.

Power, Denis "Fulacht Fiadh in County Cork", in Victor Buckley (ed.) *Burnt Offerings,* Dublin, 1990, 13-17.

Taylor, Joan J "Lunulae Reconsidered", *Proc. Prehistoric Soc.,* XXXVI, 1970, 38-81.

Bronze Age Goldwork of the British Isles. Cambridge, 1980.

Waddell, John *The Bronze Age Burials of Ireland.* Galway, 1990

Woodman, P.C. "The Early Prehistory of Munster", *J.C.H.A.S.,* LXXXIX, 1984, 1-11.

"The Mesolithic in Munster: a Preliminary Assessment" in Bonsall, Clive (ed.) *The Mesolithic in Europe.* Edinburgh, 1985.

CHAPTER TWO

Bolster, Evelyn *A History of the Diocese of Cork. From the Earliest Times to the Reformation.* Shannon, 1972.

Edwards, Nancy *The Archaeology of Early Medieval Ireland.* London, 1990.

Graham-Campbell, J.A. "Some Neglected Viking-Age Silver Hoards from near Athlone and Co. Cork", *Peritia,* 5, 1986, 309-16.

Gwynn, Aubrey and Neville Hadcock, R.

Medieval Religious Houses Ireland. Blackrock, 1988.

Hall, Richard "A Checklist of Viking-Age Coin Finds from Ireland", *Ulster Jnl. Archaeology,* 36 & 37, 1973-74, 71-86.

Jeffries, Henry A. "The History and Topography of Viking Cork", *J.C.H.A.S.,* XL, 1985, 14-25.

Lennox-Barrow, George *The Round Towers of Ireland. Dublin.* 1979.

Murphy, T.F. "A Long Cist Grave at Coppingerstown, Co. Cork", *J.C.H.A.S.,* LXIV, 1961, 65-66.

Mytum, Harold *The Origins of Early Christian Ireland.* London, 1992.

O'Kelly, M.J. "A Long Cist Grave at Hoddersfield, Co. Cork", *J.C.H.A.S.,* LX, 1955, 95-6.

O Riain, Padraig "St. Finbarr: A Study in a Cult", *J.C.H.A.S.,* LXXXII, 1977, 63-82.

Ryan, Michael (ed.) *Treasures of Ireland. Irish Art 3000 BC-1300 AD.* Dublin, 1983.

Rynne, Colin "Milling in the 7th Century-Europe's Earliest Tide-mills", *Archaeology Ireland,* vol.6, no.2, 1992, 22-24.

"Early-Medieval Horizontal-Wheeled Mill Penstocks from Co. Cork", *J.C.H.A.S.,* XCVII, 1992, 54-68.

CHAPTER THREE

Barry, T.B. *The Archaeology of Medieval Ireland.* London, 1987.

Bolster, Evelyn *A History of the Diocese of Cork. From the Earliest Times to the Reformation.* Shannon, 1972.

Candon, A. "The Cork Suburb of Dungarvan", *J.C.H.A.S.,* XC, 1986, 1-25.

Cherry, Stella (ed.) *Digging Up Cork.* Cork, 1992.

Cleary, R.M. "Medieval Town Wall off Lambley's Lane, Cork City", *J.C.H.A.S.,* XLIII, 1988, 104-08.

Hurley, M and Power, D. "The Medieval Town Wall of Cork", *J.C.H.A.S.,* LXXXVI, 1981, 1-20.

Hurley, M.F. "Wooden Artefacts from the Excavation of the Medieval City of Cork", in McGrail, Sean (ed.) *Woodworking Techniques before A.D. 1500.* B.A.R. International Series, 129, 1982, 301-11.

"Excavations of Part of the Medieval City Wall at Grand Parade, Cork", *J.C.H.A.S.,* XC, 1985, 65-90.

"Excavations in Medieval Cork: St Peter's Market", *J.C.H.A.S.,* XCI, 1986, 1-25.

"Excavations at Grand Parade, Cork II. Part 1", *J.C.H.A.S.,* XCIV, 1989, 27-45. Part 2, J.C.H.A.S., XCV, 1990, 64-87.

Jeffries, H.A. "The Founding of Anglo-Norman Cork", *J.C.H.A.S.,* XCI, 1986, 26-48.

Mc Neill, Tom *English Heritage Book of Castles.* London, 1992.

O'Kelly, Michael J. "A Shell Midden at Carrigtohill, Co. Cork", *J.C.H.A.S.,* LX, 1955, 28-32.

Thomas, Avril *The Walled Towns of Ireland.* 2 vols, Dublin, 1992.

Went, Arthur J "The Fisheries of the River Lee", *J.C.H.A.S.,* LXV, 1960, 27-35.

CHAPTER FOUR

Brunicardi, Niall *Haulbowline, Spike and Rocky Islands.* Fermoy, 1982.

Craig, Maurice *The Architecture of Ireland from the Earliest Times to 1880.* London, 1982.

Coleman, J.C. "The Old Castles Around Cork Harbour", *J.C.H.A.S.,* XX, 1914, 161-175; XXI, 1-10, 53-68, 105-12, 156-180.

Enoch, Victor J. *The Martello Towers of Ireland.* Dublin (n.d.)

Kerrigan, Paul M. "The Defences of Ireland 1793-1815; 10, Cork Harbour and Kinsale", *An Cosantoir,* February 1975, 59-63.

"Seventeenth-Century Fortifications, Forts and Garrisons in Ireland: a preliminary list", *Irish Sword,* XIV, 1980-81, 3-24.

Leask, Harold G. *Irish Castles and Castellated Houses.* Dundalk, 1986.

Monk, Judith and Tobin, Red *Barryscourt Castle: An Architectural Survey.* Cork, 1991.

Mulcahy, Michael et al. "Elizabeth Fort, Cork", *Irish Sword,* IV, 1959-60, 127-134.

Saunders, Andrew. *Fortress Britain.* Avon, 1989.

CHAPTER FIVE

Bielenberg, Andy *Cork's Industrial Revolution 1780-1880.* Cork, 1991.

Coakley, D. J. *Cork: its Trade and Commerce.* Cork, 1919.

Creedon, C *The Cork and Macroom Direct Railway.* Cork, 1960.

Cork City Railway Stations. Cork, 1986.

The Cork, Bandon and South Coast Railway, vol.1 1849-1899. Cork, 1986; vol.2 1900-1950, Cork, 1989; vol.3 1951-1961-1976, Cork, 1991.

Foley, Con *A History of Douglas.* Cork, 1981.

Jenkins, Stanley C. *The Cork and Muskerry Light Railway.* Oxford, 1992.

Lincoln, Colm *Steps and Steeples. Cork at the Turn of the Century.* Dublin, 1981.

McGrath, Walter *Tram Tracks Through Cork. Cork.* 1981.

McGuire, E.B. *Irish Whiskey.* Dublin, 1973.

O'Mahony, Colman *The Maritime Gateway to Cork.* Cork, 1986.

O'Sullivan Charles J. *The Gasmakers. Historical Perspectives on the Irish Gas Industry.* Dublin, 1987.

O'Sullivan, William *The Economic History of Cork City from the Earliest Times to the Act of Union.* Cork, 1937.

Pochin Mould, Daphne *Captain Roberts of the Sirius.* Cork, 1988.

Rynne, Colin "Cork's Industrial Past", *Technology Ireland,* March 1991, 22, 36-38.

"Two Centuries of Cork Porter", *Technology Ireland,* September 1992, 25, 30-32.

Index